"Laura Balogh and Michael A. Murray created an inclusive therapeutic program within our elementary school that enabled students to grow and thrive in classrooms and with their peers. As a retired principal of their elementary school, I am proud to recommend their book, *The Therapeutic Inclusion Program: Establishment and Maintenance in Public Schools*, to teachers and administrators. The detailed recommendations on how to support students needing a therapeutic inclusion program in public schools is a must-read for any educator, counselor, and administrator looking to create a student-centered program."

Sharon Young, *retired principal*

"*The Therapeutic Inclusion Program* by Murray and Balogh is thoughtfully and meaningfully designed. As a school administrator, I was able to 'feel' and experience the core tenets of a public school's successful therapeutic program. The reader will be able to use Murray and Balogh's book in whole or in part, based on their current needs while developing an in-district program. This is a tremendous resource for all stakeholders in the development of their own Therapeutic Inclusion Program."

Jessica Murphy, M.Ed., CAGS, *Director of Student Services*

The Therapeutic Inclusion Program

This timely guide discusses methods, organizational structures, and philosophies which can be used by school counselors, special educators, and administrators to establish therapeutic inclusion programs in K-12 schools.

The Therapeutic Inclusion Program opens with information about therapeutic classrooms and continues with explanations of how the programs function within the larger public school community. As the book travels through the therapeutic program, it discusses staff roles and qualifications, staff-to-student ratios, and the role of administration. Each chapter uses two approaches toward describing the implementation of a therapeutic inclusion program, beginning with a description of the structure and practices, along with the reasoning that supports them, and following with examples from real work experience in the form of vignettes, which will illustrate the concepts and structures in action.

Intended for education and counseling professionals looking to design, implement, and maintain an effective therapeutic inclusion program, this book helps fill a noticeable void in public education literature and know-how regarding therapeutic programming.

Michael A. Murray is a therapist and educator with specialties in school inclusion, neurodivergence, and work with children, parents, and families.

Laura Balogh is a Massachusetts-based special educator with a specialty in child-centered curriculum modification and relationship-based social–emotional learning.

The Therapeutic Inclusion Program

Establishment and Maintenance in Public Schools

Michael A. Murray and Laura Balogh

Routledge
Taylor & Francis Group
NEW YORK AND LONDON

Cover image: © Getty Images

First published 2023
by Routledge
605 Third Avenue, New York, NY 10158

and by Routledge
4 Park Square, Milton Park, Abingdon, Oxon, OX14 4RN

Routledge is an imprint of the Taylor & Francis Group, an informa business

ISBN: 978-1-032-21893-9 (hbk)
ISBN: 978-1-032-21891-5 (pbk)
ISBN: 978-1-003-27047-8 (ebk)

DOI: 10.4324/9781003270478

Typeset in Baskerville
by Newgen Publishing UK

Contents

Foreword

In this timely and desperately needed volume, Michael Murray and Laura Balogh describe a relationship-based, therapeutic approach to supporting behaviorally, socially, and emotionally troubled children within a public school setting. The inclusion model described in this book is based on one that has been successfully deployed through the Community Services Program at the Community Therapeutic Day School (CTDS) in Lexington, MA, where, until my recent retirement, I served as Clinical Director and, as such, directed our inclusion program over that time. In fact, it was through this program that I first met Michael Murray nearly two decades ago.

CTDS is a small, private therapeutic school that was founded in 1974 by Bruce Hauptman, M.D. and Nancy Fuller, M.A., LISCW. The school philosophy was based on the teachings of Donald W. Winnicott, M.D., a British psychoanalyst with whom Dr. Hauptman studied. Dr. Winnicott was an adherent of the Object Relations school of psychoanalysis that emphasized relationship as the foundation of human development. Winnicott was based at the Paddington Green Children's Hospital in London for over 40 years. He also served as a consultant to a number of therapeutic programs, including the Mulberry Bush School, one of the seminal therapeutic schools in England that was established by Barbara Docker-Drysdale. It was upon these foundations that CTDS was founded and which served as the basis for the development of our inclusion programs. In addition, as I described in *To Hold and Be Held; The Therapeutic School as a Holding Environment*, the school was also greatly influenced by the work of John Bowlby, another member of the Object Relations school in Britain, who developed the theory of attachment.

Michael Murray's experiences in the CTDS inclusion program and as a teacher in our core therapeutic educational program have informed and inspired the work described in *The Therapeutic Inclusion Program*. It was in the program detailed in this book that he met and, together, shaped a formidable team with Laura Balogh who, with over 10 years of experience shaping academic curriculum and implementing behavioral strategies, brought a vital perspective to their work. Together, they expanded on and adapted the inclusion model to create a program that met the unique demands of the children and families they served. The work they describe in this publication is a nuanced balance of theory and practice that lends itself to a very pragmatic application of a relationship-based, psychodynamic approach to perceiving, understanding, repairing and teaching children who are suffering. The degree to which they were able to integrate supports and treatment both within the school community and with families and external service providers created, what Winnicott (1965) defined as a "Holding Environment," that is, an environment in which a child feels that everyone is working in concert to hold them together and support their development. The success they had in implementing the program and the impact it had on the families, as well as their colleagues, is a testament to their persistence in the face of many challenges. The creativity, commitment, and compassion that they brought to their efforts in seeing and supporting children and their families in need suffuse every page of this book and can serve not only as an inspiration but also a detailed roadmap for those interested in implementing this approach, one that is, more than ever, urgently needed.

Daniel Reinstein

References

Reinstein, D.K. (2006). *To hold and be held; The therapeutic school as a holding environment.* Routledge.

Winnicott, D.W. (1965). *The maturational process and the facilitating environment.* Hogarth Press.

Preface

Upon establishing our own therapeutic inclusion program within a public school, with a joint background of private and public therapeutic work, and special and general education teaching in both private and public environments, we uncovered an appreciation of the rich, complex, and encompassing work that was possible together. Despite the experience that our team brought to our program, we craved a guidebook for referencing the deep and dynamic work possible within the therapeutic inclusion program. We discovered that no such volume exists, and determined we could, in fact, create that guide.

There is a strong trend toward social-emotional learning in public schools today. Programs are cropping up, yet often without the understanding and framework for what is required to develop a sustainable, rich therapeutic inclusion program. Our vision is to let our book be that guide, and to further the inclusion discourse in education for the benefit of students, families, and communities.

Acknowledgments

Thank you Caitrin Adelman, Kunjan Anjaria (1979 – 2022), Jen Baldassarre, Steve Brennan, Amy Brinn, Jan Brown (1931–2014), Dawn Burau, Dana Cohen, Amy Corral, Christine Cronin-Tocci, Shailagh Curran, Caleb Englander, Selene Gisholt, Katina Idol, Nancy Fuller, Nadine Fowler, Edward Garmey, Sophia Garmey, Bridget Glenshaw, John Glenshaw, David Harder, Bruce Hauptman (1938–2017), Priscilla Harmel, Joel Krieg, Gabrielle Ledue, Tom McCormack, Kathy Modderno, Jenn Moran, Jessica Murphy, Cristina Pachano, Donna San Antonio, Jody Scheier, Alan Shapiro, William Sharp, Adam Silk, Michelle Traverse, Olivia Von Ferstel, Sasha Watkins, and Sharon Young for your help (direct and indirect) with this book.

We would also like to thank Amanda Savage, Grace McDonnel, Katya Porter, and the team at Routledge.

Personal Acknowledgments

The philosophies and methodology described in *The Therapeutic Inclusion Program* are built upon generations of study, practice, and development. Community Therapeutic Day School (CTDS) in Lexington, Massachusetts, has been my primary learning ground, the place where I accessed an ongoing conversation. I worked or collaborated with the school over the course of 15 school years. CTDS foundationally draws on the work of British pediatrician and psychoanalyst D.W. Winnicott, and has continued to be in a forward thinking and historically informed dialogue with the psychological community. The school employs a tremendously gifted staff, prioritizing collaboration and communication, and ensuring that there is time for the exchange of ideas and perspectives.

The therapeutic inclusion program model presented in this book is based on the model I learned at CTDS. There, I learned about clinical supervision, working within a therapeutic milieu, and the value of a professional culture of communication and collaboration. I learned and developed practices for previewing and morning circle. I learned about social stories, and developed my own style of social storytelling. I coled thousands of group psychotherapy sessions with children. The school's administration, always open to innovation, was flexible and supportive as I developed a distinct approach toward group psychotherapy with children. The parent/guardian communication model, with daily communication books, weekly conversations, within a clinically supervised and collaborative philosophy, is especially specific to CTDS. The combination of these core therapeutic building blocks, and the character of the approach at the school, are carried forward in the therapeutic inclusion program.

Thank you to all of my beloved family, who love me and taught me how to be with people: My mother and father, my sisters Shelagh, Lauren, Mary, and Siobhan, my wife Debbie who believes in me and generously gives me time to write, and my fantastic children Benjamin and Rebecca.

Thank you Daniel Reinstein for being a mentor in my work as well as the truest friend.

My most valuable learning experiences are the conversations I had with students, parents, and colleagues at CTDS and other learning grounds, which include Lesley University, the Northeast Society for Group Psychotherapy, and Parenting Journey in Somerville, Massachusetts.

Michael A. Murray

My formative experiences as an educator have been rooted in child-centered philosophy, beginning with my work as an early childhood educator at Peabody Terrace Children's Center at Harvard University in Cambridge, MA. The support and guidance from Katy Donovan, Christina Cabral Punch, Cathy Durgin, and Serena Chang-Bacon guided my first years as a teacher. You stretched me to think creatively and flexibly, and to honor children—which I will take with me throughout my life and career. It was here that I also learned how to partner with parents in its truest form, and thank Jocelyn Viterna, Jason Beckfield, Carolyn Wood, Ian Sue Wing, Jocelyn Kasper, Noah Maslan, and their children for their trust in these relationships which developed into friendships.

After moving on to a public school setting, the support, mentorship, and friendship from Joanna Lieberman made me realize how to be a truly inclusive teacher.

A shift to special education was near seamless and successful with the support of great leadership, Sharon Young and Jessica Murphy, and the most devoted, knowledgeable, and caring coworkers, Nancy Boutin, Noelle Ng, and Shailagh Curran. As colleagues and administrators, you allowed me to thrive, to bring my whole and best self to my work, and let me laugh (copiously) and cry (occasionally) along the way.

I would like to extend my greatest thanks to the students who I have had the privilege to teach. Many of you have touched my heart and allowed me to become a thoughtful relationship-based educator, by bringing your authentic selves to our relationships and work together. You are why I do this work.

Thank you to my parents, Brian and JoAnne, for their unwavering support and encouragement and my sister, Hannah.

Thank you to my husband, Art, for everything, and my daughter Eleanor, may you continue to be a force in this world and encourage me to help make it a better place.

Laura Balogh

A Note on Terminology

We recognize and value the diversity of families, caretaking, and guardianship. Not everyone who does the work of parenting is a parent. When we use the word "parent" in this book, we are referring to anyone who takes on the special responsibility of ensuring that a child is cared for and loved in their home, and as they venture into the world.

Mental health professionals in school settings are generally called counselors. In this book we use both "counselor" and "therapist" to refer to the therapeutic inclusion program counselor. These two terms have somewhat different connotations. Using the term therapist at times helps to differentiate the program counselor role from a traditional school counselor role.

We use the term "therapeutic educator" to apply to any of the staff of the therapeutic inclusion program, as they are all working at the intersection of therapy and education.

In this book, we refer copiously to therapeutic supervision, and the role of a program supervisor. A program supervisor *is* a clinical supervisor, operating as a clinician for the therapeutic inclusion program. As this term and concept is largely foreign to public school staff, we have chosen to use the term "program supervisor." A program supervisor is *not* a member of the school district's administrative team, which is referred to as administrators or their specific roles of principal, assistant principal, special education coordinator, etc. throughout the book.

Introduction

The School Day Begins in the Therapeutic Inclusion Program

Welcome to school

Nicole is a second-grader at her local neighborhood elementary school. Each day her mother walks her to school. Her mother wishes her a good day near the front door, as she leaves her to enter the building and begin her day. For Nicole, there are always some worried feelings that come with entering such a big, busy, crowded place. However, she is comforted knowing that she is headed to a friendly, quiet, and cozy, specialized classroom.

Nicole is a member of a therapeutic inclusion program nested inside her neighborhood elementary school. Here this program is known as the Oak Program. Nicole is at the center of a thoughtfully designed system of care. The program provides support for Nicole's family, and for Nicole's classroom teacher through consultation and collaboration. These layers of support help her feel safe, cared for, and ready to learn.

Nicole makes her way to the familiar Oak Program classroom and is greeted by her teachers. She is seamlessly prompted and guided into greeting the other people in the room. Greeting peers and adults is an important social skill that doesn't come easily to Nicole, as well as some of her Oak Program classmates. The Oak staff is weaving this social learning throughout the day, naturally beginning with a morning hello. Ms. Kelly, an Oak staff member, reminds Nicole to check in at her larger general education classroom, and then come back for morning circle.

Nicole is able to navigate her general education classroom check-in, while not independently, with success. Nicole hangs her backpack in her locker and is prompted by Ms. Kelly to remember her homework folder. She then walks into the classroom and greets her general education teacher, Ms. Ricci, asking what the lunch choice is for the day. After completing her lunch choice and putting down her chair, Nicole looks relieved to be able to walk down the hallway back to the Oak classroom.

Nicole enters the Oak classroom, where six other Oak Program students are sitting on the floor in a circle, as well as four staff members. As a group of students with social, emotional, and behavioral difficulties, the teachers must settle, coax, and use limit-setting in order to gather the morning group. However, in short order the group is ready.

DOI: 10.4324/9781003270478-1

A remarkable gathering

The gathering of this group is remarkable in itself. Without a therapeutic inclusion program, many of the students would be scattered among various private therapeutic schools in the region.

While many private therapeutic schools are excellent, attending these schools also comes with drawbacks. Therapeutic schools are generally smaller settings, with less resources overall, and naturally necessitate withdrawal from the student's established community.

For some students a private therapeutic school is the appropriate setting. These schools have the therapeutic advantage of being a site and staff that is comprehensively designed for, and dedicated to, the therapeutic care of students who require it. Some students need a level of consistency and shared mission that can only be developed in such a setting.

A well organized and maintained therapeutic inclusion program cannot entirely replace the need for placements in private settings. However, a quality program will be an appropriate fit for many students, who may have needed a private placement in the absence of such a program.

Nicole is just such a student. She will receive the therapeutic care she needs within her own school community, along with all of the general resources it contains. The school community gains from the program as well, by housing a sophisticated therapeutic inclusion program and all the diversity of students and professional skills that come with it.

Authenticity and relationships are foundational

The therapeutic inclusion program is built upon authentic and caring relationships. Morning circle is how the program models these values at the start of each day. Everyone is greeted to start the morning circle, and classic elementary school daily rituals are completed such as the calendar and day of school. The experience becomes more personalized as the day is previewed along with individual details, as well as any events coming up in the days ahead. The goal is for the students to feel informed and respected.

All the staff and students are given an opportunity to share any news they feel the group should know before morning circle concludes. Nicole shares that her sister's birthday is tomorrow, which leads to a short discussion about Nicole's family's plans to celebrate.

After morning circle, Nicole stops by her Monday schedule, an individualized, visual schedule, posted in a consistent location on the classroom wall. This combination of previewing and math curriculum (calendar and days of school) is happening concurrently in their larger general education classroom. In the smaller program group, a more personalized approach is possible.

Nicole has an Oak Program classmate named Amir. They attend the same second-grade general education class. Now that morning circle is over, Nicole, Amir, and Ms. Kelly leave the Oak classroom. They make their way to the second-grade general education classroom, Ms. Ricci's class. This is the inclusion environment. Nicole, Amir, and Ms. Kelly are greeted by Ms. Ricci and join in with the math lesson that is about to begin. Ms. Kelly has developed a working partnership with Ms. Ricci and is able to help throughout the classroom while ensuring that Nicole and Amir get the support they need.

Laying the groundwork

Nicole is about 25 minutes into her school day, and core components of a successful therapeutic inclusion program are already at work.

The program has a safe, warm, and friendly home base. This is the Oak classroom, the therapeutic inclusion program's center. Many students depend on this home base in order to make safe excursions into the larger school. This is analogous to a young child exploring and then returning to their parent, as described by Margaret Mahler in The Psychological Birth of the Human Infant (1975). Like the young child, our students are able to explore the more complex and less predictable social world of the school, because they know they will return to check back with their home base.

Oak morning circle provides previewing, connection, the communication of respect and authenticity through the sharing of information and by ensuring that students are heard.

A quick preview of the important relationship between the general education lead classroom teacher Ms. Ricci and the supporting inclusion program staff member Ms. Kelly was shown. An all-in-this-together approach allows the two educators to fully integrate the classroom. Both Ms. Ricci and Ms. Kelly are ready to work with the whole class, while the two teachers make sure everyone's needs are met.

Our therapeutic inclusion program students are in their home community, which is of tremendous value both to the students and the community at large. The community adds to the richness of these student's experiences. Simultaneously, the school community is enhanced due to the diversity of students included. The therapeutic inclusion program is at the frontline of deep social, emotional, and behavioral work. The program staff, operating from a deeply therapeutic perspective, provides the school with another resource for learning and problem-solving.

There is nearly a full day of school remaining, and the seeds have been planted for an educational and therapeutic day for Nicole. The following chapters will describe the themes touched upon in this introduction in greater detail, as well as additional aspects of the therapeutic inclusion program.

Reference

Mahler, M. S., Pine, F., & Bergman, A. (1975). *The psychological birth of the human infant: Symbiosis and individuation*. Basic Books.

1 The Therapeutic Program Classroom

The therapeutic program classroom is the program's center within the school. The classroom's location within a general education school provides a remarkable social/emotional learning opportunity. Skills and understanding in social and emotional domains are explicitly developed, discussed, and practiced there. These understandings and skills can then be exported to the general education environment. New or challenging social and academic situations are often both previewed and reviewed in the therapeutic classroom. Planning, previewing, and making time for "how did it go?" are all valuable to the process.

The therapeutic program classroom is a therapeutic milieu. The philosophy that guides the classroom environment and the structure of the classroom are described in this chapter. The story of a student named Amir is shared to illustrate how a secure home base within the school can provide the sense of safety necessary for social, emotional, and academic progress.

A secure home base

Developmental psychologist Mary Ainsworth recognized that every person needs a secure home base in order to develop (1978). Fellow foundational attachment theorist John Bowlby explained: "Unless a therapist can enable his patient to feel some measure of security, therapy cannot even begin" (1988, p. 159). Most working adults tolerate difficult days at their jobs, because they know they will eventually return home. Most children are able to make it through long days at school because they will eventually return to their familiar home and family. For our students on a different trajectory of emotional and social development, a school day is much too long to wait.

For many students, once acclimated, the crowded classrooms and hallways may appear familiar, and possibly even full of social opportunity. For our therapeutic inclusion program students, the crowds and commotion of the public school feel too unpredictable, too noisy, and too chaotic. Anxiety grows, taking up more and more cognitive real estate. With anxiety taking over, our students can increasingly feel limited to a few socially maladaptive behaviors in order to try to manage an overwhelming environment.

They return to habits and reactions that have served them well in delivering them from desperate circumstances, and into engagement with a reliable adult.

DOI: 10.4324/9781003270478-2

These can include screaming, running, yelling, pushing, and finding a conflict. These solutions may get them the support they need in the moment, but do not promote growth and a sense of personal accomplishment.

The therapeutic inclusion program classroom is the secure home base—the reliably safe place—for our students. In our school, we call it the Oak classroom, or just Oak. The Oak classroom features a smaller group of students, and a high teacher-to-student ratio. In our experience, seven students is a good number for a therapeutic classroom, with two therapeutic educators present. (A *therapeutic educator* is any staff member working at the intersection of therapy and education, including the staff of the therapeutic inclusion program.) It's a room where people are encouraged to share, to be curious, and where checking in about emotional well-being is normal and routine.

In the Oak classroom, we have the flexibility, resources, staff, and training necessary to respond individually and patiently to the social, emotional, and behavioral issues that arise. Students in the program quickly learn that the Oak classroom is a place to take refuge, to have feelings, and to get support. It is also a place where positive memories are built through relationship-building activities and accumulated time together. A sense of security develops when teachers are curious and caring, and when teachers have the precious resources of time and attention to share with a small group of students. In this way, the therapeutic inclusion program classroom becomes the students' secure home base within the school.

The work of pediatrician and psychoanalyst D.W. Winnicott and his concept of the "holding environment" are central to the approach of the therapeutic inclusion program. The holding environment is a responsive relationship created by the caretaker of an infant or young child, where anxiety-provoking impingements are kept to a minimum (1965, p. 47). Winnicott focuses on the relationships that are formed from infancy as babies are kept safe and cared for in the arms of their parents. This is the initial holding environment, though it evolves as the child matures. The infant is first held in their parent's arms, then they are held between their parents and the child's exploration of the world, followed by being held within the triangular relationships within a family and community (Winnicott, 1965, pp. 181–183).

For a range of reasons, the emotional and social maturities of our therapeutic inclusion program students are delayed, and so they require a more sensitive and responsive holding environment. This smaller and exquisitely responsive environment is designed to afford our students the necessary sense of safety and security in order to continue their exploration of the world.

The name Oak was chosen chiefly as an aspect of maintaining a secure base. Oak is a non-stigmatizing word. It does not identify the social, emotional, and behavioral challenges of the students. It does not carry any therapeutic or educational associations at all.

Once the therapeutic inclusion program classroom is established as a secure home base, it becomes a source of courage for the program student. At the developmental stage where we meet students in elementary school, they have expanded beyond the holding environment of the embrace of their caretaker in infancy, and beyond the toddler stage of short excursions within close range of their caretakers. Their holding environment can be within the triangular relationships of a small community, if it is sufficiently attuned and responsive. The therapeutic inclusion program classroom contains and symbolically represents this small community. The classroom, and the community it represents, functions in the same way that a parent functions for a toddler as the child separates and explores the room. The child knows their parent is nearby, and they will return to their parent. This knowledge gives the child the confidence to explore (Mahler et al., 1975).

In much the same way, our students in the Oak Program draw confidence from the therapeutic program classroom. Knowing that they have a safe retreat makes the hallway less anxiety provoking, and the general education classroom more tolerable. With their anxiety reduced through their confidence that there is a secure base nearby, there is cognitive and emotional space to try new things, and step away from maladaptive established habits.

Winnicott theorized that in order to have healthy development the infant requires a holding environment provided by their caretaker, which protects them from the "unthinkable anxieties" (1965, pp. 57—58). Winnicott's unthinkable anxieties are "1) Going to pieces. 2) Falling forever. 3) Having no relationship to the body. 4) Having no orientation" (p. 58). These are existential concerns, and these existential concerns continue to underlie the anxieties of our students struggling with school socially and emotionally. Analogous to the infant's caretaker warding off the unthinkable anxieties by holding the baby and being attuned and responsive to the needs of the infant, the therapeutic inclusion program maintains an environment for the student which is highly responsive and attuned. Through this we are able to support the social and emotional maturation of the child.

The therapeutic milieu

The therapeutic inclusion program is able to create and maintain the secure base by operating the program classroom as a therapeutic milieu. The word "milieu" is used rather flexibly by different professionals. For our purposes, a therapeutic milieu is a responsive environment, grounded in psychological principles including empathy, maintenance of boundaries, transference and countertransference, and attunement to both the individual and group. In order to facilitate a responsive and cohesive therapeutic milieu, the staff must meet regularly, separate from the students. In these meetings the program staff discusses developments, responses, and their own reactions to what is transpiring in the group. This is mostly achieved through the practice of supervision, as practiced by mental health professionals, as a crucial and necessary component of quality therapeutic work. In most mental health work, while staff collaboration and communication is ongoing, a weekly time is set aside explicitly for supervision.

Identifying and operating the classroom as a therapeutic milieu reinforces the importance of the program's work within emotional and social realms. It is easy in the school environment for both students and staff to get subsumed into the push for academic productivity and progress. In most cases for students in the therapeutic inclusion program, academic productivity and progress are only possible once they feel that school is a safe-enough and predictable-enough place for them to shift some of their attention away from self-protective vigilance, and toward academic learning.

A core understanding, especially within the therapeutic milieu, is that the therapeutic work is ongoing and always occurring. The therapeutic work and approach are not confined to special times or activities. When a student who has had a very difficult time being and feeling accomplished at school is engaged in successful academic learning, this too is therapy for the child. This is part of a reparative school experience.

It is understood by the group that within the program classroom, we will take time and attention to focus on emotional well-being, and interpersonal dynamics. If we choose to, we can press the "pause button" on any activity in order to address social and emotional well-being. From social interactions, to anxiety around academic work, teachable moments abound within the therapeutic classroom. The program staff use these moments to move the therapeutic work forward, and support adaptive maturation.

There is also a daily 30-minute session that is dedicated explicitly to the therapeutic development of the students. Group psychotherapy can be daily during this time. If the program wants to reserve some time for a more instructional approach to social skills, then a model with three group psychotherapy sessions, and two social skills groups per week can function well. In the tradition of Community Therapeutic Day School in Lexington, Massachusetts, group psychotherapy is informally called *meeting*. During group psychotherapy, there is an understanding that emotional, social, and behavioral issues will be discussed and worked on together, and there is an explicit and shared understanding of confidentiality. While the program classroom is generally a welcoming place to the school community, during group psychotherapy the door is closed and there are no interruptions. This time is a tremendous opportunity to work with the social, emotional, and behavioral issues presenting within the group, which naturally echo the same difficulties which brought our students to the program. Meeting will be discussed in more detail in Chapter Three.

Unfortunately, in our experience many programs in public schools which use the title *therapeutic* do not actually incorporate core therapeutic tenets, such as the supervision model. Instead, many implement practices from the behaviorist realm of therapeutic work, without a foundation of fundamental therapeutic concepts and practices. Chapter Nine of this book will describe the supervision model that supports the therapeutic work, in detail.

A reparative school experience

Most often, by the time a student has been placed in a therapeutic inclusion program, there has been some injury to the student–school relationship.

Teachers are, by and large, remarkably caring and kind people. In most cases, prior to joining the therapeutic inclusion program, there has been a mismatch.

Usually the mismatch is in the relationship of the student's needs to the school's resources and environment. The student-to-teacher ratio may be too large given the developmental stage of the child. The teacher and staff may not have the mental health expertise necessary to care for a student. The organization of the classroom may be age-appropriate for most students, but not predictable and organized enough for a student with severe anxiety, for example. A specific teacher–student relationship can certainly mitigate or exacerbate a situation, but outside extreme circumstances, the teacher–student relationship is not the root issue.

The weight of the mismatch is felt by the student, the teachers, the parents, and others. It is usually the vulnerable student who is most impacted. A sense of social and academic failure can be internalized rather quickly, especially in these early formative years. School becomes a distressing place. In response to the child's developmental inclination to develop a sense of ability and control, school becomes the enemy.

In the therapeutic milieu of the Oak classroom, the staff seeks to form a different kind of teacher–student relationship with the child. In this relationship, the emotional well-being of the child can be prioritized ahead of any academic concerns.

Given the student's experiences, our status as school staff often means that the student starts from a place of distrust. From that position, it is the therapeutic educator's task to build trust, build a safe relationship, and facilitate positive experiences together at school.

Often, as time passes and healing occurs, the student comes to believe that there is something different and special about the therapeutic teachers—or sometimes about just one therapeutic teacher with whom they are initially able to form a relationship. This is the reparative relationship, discussed further in Chapter Five.

Perhaps the most significant piece of the repair is the student learning that it is possible to grow, flourish, and feel good about themselves at school. Further into the repair students look beyond the program for supportive relationships. They learn that when they have the security necessary to look, they will find many safe, caring, and supportive educators throughout schools. These principles are illustrated in Amir's story.

Amir

Amir met Mr. Twomey in his public school's extended school year program as a rising first grader. It was a 15-day summer program, designed to help students maintain social skills. Amir was an ebullient, radiant child, with delayed development of social awareness, social skills, and emotional regulation. Mr. Twomey was a counselor, who would be co-leading the therapeutic inclusion program in the fall.

Mr. Twomey learned from Amir's general education kindergarten teacher that he had struggled to adapt at the beginning of his kindergarten school year. But over time, Amir acclimated to his teacher's highly structured style, which allowed him to internalize the predictable schedule and expectations leading to an overall successful school year.

Extended school year

Mr. Twomey was co-teaching with another counselor, Ms. James, in the district's extended school year social skills program with a group of six that included Amir. Considering the 15-day duration of the summer program, time for adaptation and warming up was limited. Amir's struggles began at the start of each day, when Ms. James would facilitate a share time. Students could bring something from home to show to the group. Amir was very excited to show the other students the action figures he loved to play with, but also deeply afraid that another group member might touch his toys. His inability to reliably predict or control the behavior of his peers caused him to be very upset. He would tantrum with screaming, crying, and spastic bodily convulsions. His tantrums were so prolonged and intense, that Ms. James was concerned that Amir was having a break with reality. The reaction was in fact the response of a child deeply overwhelmed by a new environment and set of expectations.

Over the course of 15 days, Mr. Twomey progressively helped Amir acclimate to the daily schedule, starting from the beginning. With careful previewing, Amir adapted to the morning share, then to the first daily lesson, and they worked their way through the entire schedule over the course of approximately 10 days. Unfortunately, by the time Amir had adapted to the routines, the summer program had just about concluded.

Entering first grade

Come September and a new school year, having successfully navigated kindergarten, Amir was placed in a first-grade general education classroom with an experienced teacher. The hope and expectation was, while being provided with a continuation of special education services, that he would continue with overall success, similar to his kindergarten experience. However, given the increased social and academic demands of first grade, Amir was not able to adequately adjust.

The therapeutic inclusion program classroom, the Oak Program, was just around the corner from Amir's first-grade general education classroom. While Amir was not yet a member of the program, Mr. Twomey frequently heard and sometimes witnessed his deep upsets and tantrums. He often had his tantrums in the hallway outside his first-grade classroom. Amir's tantrums always included screaming, and often included spitting, eating paper, and drawing on his own face and skin with markers or pen.

Mr. Twomey had some circumstantial opportunities to observe Amir with his class. What struck him most was Amir's deep agitation. Amir was on high alert, highly anxious, and deeply frustrated with his school situation. It was not surprising he was having conflicts with his peers, and frequently struggling with school staff.

Peers complained about Amir getting physical with them at recess, where he would run zigzags across the play area. Mr. Twomey noticed that the more agitated Amir appeared, the closer he would get to his peers while running through the group. Teachers encountered a student who might dig in his heels at any moment and refuse to follow any directions. Amir was not able to understand what was expected of him at school, and unable to predict the behavior of those around him. As a result he was highly anxious and very unhappy.

Placement in the therapeutic inclusion program

After eight weeks of school it was determined by Amir's Individual Education Program (IEP) team, which included his mother, that he would join the therapeutic inclusion program—the Oak Program. A carefully thought out and phased transition was planned for Amir, and carried out. Parent communication between the program and Amir's mother was established. Copious previewing was done for the program group, and for Amir.

Using colorful and illustrated social stories, Amir was introduced to morning circle and its careful, thorough, and individualized previewing. Amir learned about the Oak Program's counseling groups: meeting (group psychotherapy) and group (social skills building lessons and activities). Once in the Oak classroom, Amir started to develop new and often playful relationships with teachers and peers in the program. In the Oak classroom he experienced new and fun personal connections in a more predictable environment, along with more consistent responses to his tantrums. Program staff developed an individualized behavior intervention plan to help him adapt to using the new space available. Amir continued to attend lessons in his general education classroom as well, with support from Oak staff.

As the program's work with Amir developed, he began to rely on the Oak classroom as a safe place to be upset. The program classroom also encompassed a smaller room right next door, referred to as the Oak office. For Amir, this smaller space became a safe place to have his tantrums. With supervision from an Oak staff member, Amir could have his feelings without anyone needing to be concerned that he was disrupting other learners. This was a massive improvement over the hallway, which was stigmatizing for Amir and disruptive for his schoolmates.

Amir's development of a safe place to be upset was a very significant improvement for him. Understandably, school staff had tried to set limits on Amir's behavior when his tantrums were in the hallway. It was surely difficult for Amir to make a distinction between his behavior requiring limits and the sense that his feelings were unacceptable. By developing a safe place to express his feelings, the Oak classroom and office, Amir learned that his feelings were accepted and welcome. While the therapeutic inclusion program worked to get this message across to Amir, he channeled those feelings into safer but still cathartic behaviors within the Oak office.

Amir needed ongoing work to develop safe behaviors during his tantrums, even within the confines of the private room. His habitualized upset behaviors of eating paper, spitting, and drawing on his skin took time to diminish and replace with more adaptive responses to agitation. Oak staff worked collaboratively and creatively to support him.

Relationship-based change

The therapeutic work that takes place within the therapeutic inclusion program is foremost relationship-based. Behavioral approaches are used, but only within the context of established therapeutic relationships. The program's first task with Amir was to establish a relationship, with care and reliability.

In order to form a relationship Oak staff set reliable limits and boundaries, while simultaneously looking for every opportunity to be playful, flexible, attuned to the individual, and nurturing. Once the relationship is adequately established, individual behavior plans can be established when appropriate.

In Amir's case, he earned a reward for using the calm down space when he chose to, or was directed to. Amir was very responsive to the relationship-based introduction and the subsequent implementation of a reward system. Over a period of weeks he developed a simple routine where he would go to the small room when he was upset, and sit in a particular chair for five minutes, using a timer. Usually one five-minute session would do, but sometimes he needed more. Sometimes he would yell in the chair, sometimes he would turn himself upside down in the chair, but it was safe and he would move on when he was done.

At the same time, Amir was developing positive and fun relationships within the Oak Program. He responded very well to the attentive and often playful classroom atmosphere. He loved to draw, and to share his latest drawings with his Oak classmates and teachers. In the Oak classroom Amir had found a place to play, a safe way to be upset, and a reliable place to look for support. He had found his secure base within the large public school.

The establishment of a secure base had a profound effect on Amir's ability to engage both academically and socially in the general education environments of the school. Amir's general level of agitation decreased dramatically. A sweet and good-natured child who loved to have fun was able to emerge. He stopped getting physical with his peers at recess. Teachers found that Amir was now able to follow directions.

When his general education teacher dropped a paper, Amir had the mental and emotional space available to notice and respond. He went over quickly to pick it up and hand it to her. Based on her previous experience with Amir, she was both surprised and moved by the gesture.

What Mr. Twomey found most noticeable about Amir's progress was the lifting of his agitation. Amir had found the first-grade general education environment to be confusing and overwhelming. He had been deeply unhappy, and he had been communicating his unhappiness to everyone around him through his behaviors. Once Amir established a refuge within the school building in the secure base of the Oak Program classroom, his anxiety lifted. With the weight of his agitation no longer draped over him, a playful, happy, and ready-to-learn child emerged.

Academic progress in the program classroom

Fundamental to the mission of the therapeutic inclusion program is that academic progress is only possible when our students feel secure enough to cognitively attend to the task of academic learning. Oftentimes the therapeutic inclusion program classroom is the first place where they feel enough security, and are able to more fully engage in curriculum.

In fact, while the therapeutic inclusion program classroom serves the many purposes outlined, it is most frequently used for instruction. Program staff provide all manner of modified and accommodated curriculum individually and in small groups. The program staff is experienced and prepared in providing curriculum and remediation. Reading and math instruction make up most of the program room instructional time.

The room is also used for accommodated instruction when the general education environment is sensorily or socially overwhelming. Depending on a number of factors, from the time of day, to the activity at hand, some of our students need a smaller group in order to access a learning activity. One or two students from the general education classroom can join in a small learning group in the Oak classroom. This provides students with learning peers, helps to integrate the program into the school in general, allows some general education students to have additional targeted instruction in their school learning experience, and provides extra teacher attention.

Physical structure of the classroom

The Oak classroom provides a good model for what a therapeutic inclusion program classroom should look like.

Therapeutic inclusion program students are "dual citizens." They are full members of the general education classrooms, and also members of the therapeutic inclusion program. As such, they have their own established personal spaces in both environments. In their general education classrooms they have desks with storage inside, cubbies, and sometimes other organizational systems. In the therapeutic inclusion classroom, each student has their own desk with storage inside. The student's name is clearly labeled on the desk. Having a place all one's own within the therapeutic classroom encourages a sense of belonging and ownership.

Personalized daily schedules are posted on the wall, spread out so students can look at their own, without extraneous information (see Figure 2.1 in Chapter 2: Sample daily schedule). Schedules are written on laminated cardstock so that they can be updated with a whiteboard marker to reflect schedule changes, and are flippable so only one day at a time is visible. This helps reduce the amount of information the child has to take in. Only the current day's relevant information is visible. The schedules are color coded to denote whether activities are taking place in the student's general education classroom or within the Oak classroom.

The classroom is large enough to provide some personal space to the students, room for instruction, and a calm down space. The Oak Program classroom has two kidney-shaped tables that are most useful for academic instruction. There is also a circular table toward the center of the room that is used for various purposes, and is always the location of meeting. While group psychotherapy is traditionally done seated in a circle without other furniture, younger students benefit from the way that a circular table helps to organize the space. It also provides students with a wider range of appropriate options for positioning their bodies, such as leaning on the table, or putting hands on the table.

Computers are available in the Oak classroom. However, given our student's need for social practice, we cultivate a classroom culture where computers are not frequently used, nor in-demand for rewards or breaks. There is also a teacher desk, which is of course useful organizationally, and provides a classic physical metaphor for the maintenance, and sometimes negotiation, of limits and boundaries.

A source of courage

A therapeutic inclusion program classroom that is operated as a therapeutic milieu, staffed by trained adults in close communication, dedicated to providing a reparative school experience for our students, will become a source of security and courage for program students in the public school environment. The classroom should be thoughtfully located within the school, and arranged in order to feel useful, safe, and fun for the students. Teachers should be prepared to make adaptations to the classroom in response to what is presented by the current group. This foundational space will serve as the wellspring of the therapeutic progress that supports our students, and the program's positive therapeutic influence can extend throughout the school building.

References

Ainsworth, M. (1978). *Patterns of attachment.* Routledge.

Bowlby, J. (1988). *A secure base: Parent-child attachment and healthy human development.* Basic Books.

Mahler, M. S., Pine, F., & Bergman, A. (1975). *The psychological birth of the human infant: Symbiosis and individuation.* Basic Books.

Winnicott, D. W. (1968). *The child, the family, and the outside world.* Penguin Books.

Winnicott, D. W. (1965). *The maturational processes and the facilitating environment: Studies in the theory of emotional development.* International Universities Press.

2 Morning Circle

An Expression of Respect

Beginning the day

Morning circle should occur as the student's first block of the school day, yet given the logistical complications of students arriving to school, it may not happen *immediately*. More secure students will feel comfortable enough to walk to their general education room, greet their teachers and peers, and then come to the therapeutic inclusion classroom for morning circle. Other students may feel more comfortable beginning their day in the therapeutic milieu.

Given the repetitive nature of school, students generally find themselves in a routine, beginning either in the therapeutic inclusion room or in their general education classroom. However, there is room for flexibility as students develop independence or have periods of higher need. Some students will desire to begin their day in the general education room but need the support of a program staff member in order to do so. This is an accommodation that can be provided by having a staff member meet the student in the hallway or in the classroom and, when appropriate, provide scaffolding for the student to eventually become independent in the morning.

Once students have completed their individual morning routine in their general education classroom, they go to the therapeutic inclusion classroom for morning circle. Morning circle should start around the same time each day, but it should not begin until all members are present.

In a typical general education environment, students will complete morning work during the downtime while they are waiting for all of their peers to arrive for the day and for instruction to begin. This is not recommended in the milieu of the therapeutic inclusion program. The time is used for students to connect to one another and to the program staff. This is mostly done through casual chatting and play. Students may also play with games or toys for a few minutes if they can be easily picked up and put away. If it feels necessary to provide more structure during this period of time, students can be given the option to read, draw, or play at their own space at their desks, while staff members greet and connect with students. With most groups, this time can be largely unstructured and serve as a soft landing at school after the transition from home.

Though it may not be visible to most people the program staff is busy and engaged with important therapeutic work at the very beginning of the day

DOI: 10.4324/9781003270478-3

while greeting, chatting, and playing. Staff members are attuning to individual and group presentations within the program. The first step is the visual scan upon first seeing the student. Are they neat or disheveled compared to their norm? What is their body language? What kind of expression is on their face? This information will inform the way that we greet them so that we can start from a place of attunement. As students enter the room and interact with each other we quickly get a sense for the social and emotional tenor of the group.

For the day ahead, these early moments are often both formative and informative. As staff members, we are also members of the group community and contribute to the group dynamics and emotional tenor. Is this a moment to support an interaction?—Offer positive influence?—Provide more structure?—Become quiet and unobtrusive to stay out of the way of positive student-to-student play and connection? People with strong social intelligence do many of these things naturally. In caring for the student population of the therapeutic inclusion program, these tasks are necessary and therapeutically informed.

Morning circle components

Once all members have arrived in the classroom, students should be given a heads-up that they have one or two minutes to finish up what they are doing in order to be ready for morning circle. Morning circle should be led by one consistent staff member to the extent possible. This contributes to the sense of routine as students begin their day. In a manner analogous to the structure of the therapeutic program itself, morning circle is a predictable routine designed to contain and process uncertainty and unforeseen developments. The pace and content of morning circle should also be consistent and include: (1) greeting, (2) calendar, (3) specialist teachers, (4) news from staff, and (5) news from students.

In the primary grades, morning circle typically will occur sitting on the rug with staff interspersed among the students. However, social distancing has proven that this model can be adapted quite easily to students sitting at their desks.

Students should be given the opportunity to greet one another each morning. Individual greetings aid in creating a welcoming atmosphere. In structuring the **greeting,** the school culture as a whole should be taken into consideration. If the school that you are working in utilizes a specific curriculum, such as Responsive Classroom®, this is a good opportunity to tie into the larger school community. Depending on the ages and developmental stages of students in the program, the teacher can provide an appropriate amount of structure. For young students, the teacher might lead with "today we are going to give a wave and say 'good morning' to the person next to us, around the circle." Practicing these greetings in the therapeutic milieu will prepare students to be able to engage with these greetings appropriately in their general education classroom community, and more casually throughout the school (Kriete & Davis, 2014).

After the greeting, students should be oriented to a student-friendly **calendar**. Students can be asked to provide the date in a day, month, number, and year format. In addition to the academic reinforcement that this provides, it is helpful to foster a conceptual understanding of the calendar for planning and previewing purposes. The more solid a student's concept of time is, the more they will be able to benefit from the previewing that occurs within the therapeutic milieu.

After reviewing the calendar, students should be told who their **specialist teachers** will be that day. Quite often, students who are members of therapeutic inclusion programs receive wrap-around support from specialists including, but not limited to, an occupational therapist, speech and language pathologist, board-certified behavior analyst (BCBA), and occasionally a physical therapist. Individual student plans for specialist teachers for the day are reviewed here, which helps both the student and the group anticipate these transitions. Students will be reminded of which teacher they will be seeing that day, at what time, and whether the location will be the therapeutic inclusion classroom, their general education classroom, or that teacher's office.

Following specialist teachers, any additional **news from staff** for the day should be reviewed. A whiteboard with the date and any news from that day should be included. The purpose of the explicit discussion of the day's news is to create a culture that acknowledges that there is a wide range of activities that impact a student's day. Within the therapeutic milieu, morning announcements are often more encompassing and thorough than what one would expect in a general education classroom. Any absences of students or staff should be written, any changes to the typical schedule, academic assessments, and anything else that is known and will impact any of the student's day should be written on the board. The teacher running the morning circle should review these changes and ask students if they have any follow-up questions specifically about these changes for the day.

The teacher should then preview any upcoming changes for the next few days or weeks. Students do not need to remember these changes in advance, but it is important that they are previewed and then reviewed as they get closer. It is extremely helpful to keep a month-by-month calendar near the morning circle area. This calendar does not need to be accessible to students, but staff can write any events that may be coming up such as absences, appointments, visitors to the classroom, field trips, tests, and so on. Previewing during morning circle allows the whole group, students and teachers together, to connect about the day and what to be prepared for. The intention is not simply previewing, but promoting a sense that as important members of the classroom community, they are in the know.

After all of the teacher-led portions of morning circle are complete, there is an opportunity to ask if there is **news from students**. It is helpful to ask "Is there anything that you need us to know about you today?" Students may share how they are feeling, if they have a special pick-up plan, if something exciting is happening soon such as a relative visiting, or something that they are worried about such as a doctor's appointment after school.

This is a great opportunity for students to be heard and feel understood. Student's ability to share what feels significant to them, and the staff's compassionate response paves the way for the therapeutic and educational work ahead. If a student shares at morning circle that they are tired, a thoughtful response could be "Thanks for letting me know. We'll take it a little easy this morning." The student then knows that you are respecting how they feel and are going to take their current state into consideration. This sets up a positive interaction for the following work period of the day and continues to build the relationship between the student and staff member. This daily routine illustrates an orientation toward honesty and authenticity crucial for relationship-based therapeutic work.

A morning circle in the Oak classroom

9:15 approaches and it's almost time for morning circle to begin. Three third-grade students, Henry, Anthony, and Charles, are already in the Oak classroom. Two of the students, Henry and Anthony, are playing with action figures in the classroom's cozy corner.

The cozy corner of the classroom is multipurpose. It is equipped with bean bags, pillows, blankets, and stuffed animals. Students use this as a place to calm down in the classroom if they are becoming escalated. It is a student-directed choice to utilize the cozy corner in this way, but staff in the program will, at times, make this suggestion for students who they feel would benefit at the moment. Students may use this area when they are tired or sad and need a comfortable place to rest or check in with a teacher. They will also relax and play there during downtime. That is how Henry and Anthony are using the cozy corner this morning.

Henry asks Ms. LaChance, an Oak paraprofessional, if she will come over and play action figures with them, they need a Thor. Ms. LaChance approaches, sits down with the students, and begins to play.

The therapist in the program, Mr. Twomey, is spending this time reading students' communication books. Henry, Anthony, and Charles have put their books in the inbox where they have been coached to come in and store them each day. (These books with information written from home will be circulated to the other staff members of the Oak Program.) Charles, a newer member of the Oak Program who recently moved into the district, is currently spending all of his time at school in the Oak room. He took his communication book out and put it in the inbox before taking out his laptop and headphones to listen to music as a calming way to begin his day. He references a document on his Google Classroom™ with Oak-curated links to songs to listen to, many of which were his personal requests.

At this time Nicole, a second-grade student, walks down from her general education classroom. She has her communication book, which she puts into the inbox. She asks one of the paraprofessionals, Ms. Kelly, to go to the Oak office so that they can check in privately about something that has happened on the bus. Nicole trusts Ms. Kelly, and their schedule gives them a significant amount of time together during the school day. Ms. Kelly agrees and asks if her classmates, Amir and Ava, are at school that day. Nicole responds that they are, but they are still down in Mrs. Ricci's second-grade classroom.

The special educator in the Oak classroom, Mrs. Tabor, then walks down to Mrs. Ricci's classroom to check in with the two remaining Oak members, and move them along to the Oak room for morning circle. When she arrives in Mrs. Ricci's room, Amir is still unpacking his backpack and completing his morning routine. Ava is in tears, but checking in with Mrs. Ricci. Amir receives some help to finish up his morning routine, remember his communication book, and walk down to the Oak classroom for morning circle. Mrs. Tabor then checks in with Mrs. Ricci, who gives her a quick rundown on what has been going on with Ava, and takes over comforting her. Ava articulates that she is sad, but does not have any additional information to provide about her current emotional state. This is not unusual for her. She agrees to walk together to the Oak room for morning circle, and that they can check in again afterward to see how she is doing.

Once Ava and the special educator return to the Oak classroom, the paraprofessional and Nicole have finished their check-in in the Oak office, and everyone else has received a two-minute warning that morning circle is about to begin. The students all clean up, with some prompting from the staff, and come to the circle to get ready to start the daily greeting.

The school that the Oak Program is housed in utilizes the Responsive Classroom® curriculum. In order to best prepare the students in the program to be able to actively participate in the routines taught in the curriculum in their general education classrooms, the Oak room practices Responsive Classroom® greetings during their morning circle. The group operates on a rotating schedule of choosing the greeting, and today it is Ava's turn. She chooses a simple wave greeting, and the group waves hello to each of their members.

After the greeting, Mrs. Tabor directs the student's attention to the calendar. She asks students who would like to share the date today. Many students raise their hands. Mrs. Tabor calls on Nicole. Nicole shares the date, while independently reminding the group that Wednesday means that it's an early release day. Another student, Amir, asks how many days until the weekend, as he has special plans with his grandmother that he is excited about. Nicole raises her hand to tell Amir that it is two more school days and then the weekend.

Mrs. Tabor then shares the specialist teacher schedule for the day, reminding third graders Henry and Anthony that the occupational therapist will come to Ms. Chen's class to help them with their writing at 1:30. They will continue to work on typing their narrative pieces. Amir is told that he will go and see the speech and language pathologist at 2:00. At this point, Amir expresses his displeasure about this, sharing that

"I don't want to go with Mrs. Quinn, I want to stay in my classroom." Mrs. Tabor takes a minute to ask Amir about how he's feeling and he explains that it feels too hard when he goes to Mrs. Quinn's room. Mrs. Tabor then volunteers to walk Amir to his session with Mrs. Quinn and help explain that their time together is feeling hard. Amir agrees that this would be helpful, Mrs. Tabor notes it on her calendar, and morning circle continues.

Mrs. Tabor then looks to the whiteboard where the news for the current day has been written. All students and staff related to the program are present that day, but there is a math assessment in second grade that students are made aware of. Amir, Nicole, and Ava are reminded that they will have a "math check-in" later that day that they will complete in the Oak classroom. They are reminded that when they complete a check-in that it's just for teachers to understand what kids know, so that teachers will know what to teach, and also that teachers won't be able to help them as much as they usually do during math. These three students seem to be okay with this idea.

The group then looks ahead to the remainder of the week. The students are reminded that one of the paraprofessionals in the Oak classroom will be leaving early on Friday, and that next Tuesday the third graders have a field trip. There are not any questions about this news, and so the students are asked if there's anything that they need their teachers to know about them today. On this day, many students take this time to present various news to the group. Ava tells the group that she is tired today, and as she does Amir hand signals "me too," which is commonly used and understood throughout the school. The teacher tells both students "Thanks for letting us know. Keep us updated on how you're feeling as the day goes on. We'll take it a little easy this morning."

Amir raises his hand to tell us that his grandmother is coming for the weekend. She plans to take him to Target and buy a toy and he's very excited about it. Though this may seem mundane and not applicable "news," this is on the forefront of Amir's mind. Amir tends to perseverate on toys and events. In order to help him work through these moments, it is important that his teachers are well aware and can help hold his anticipatory excitement and anxiety. As the day progresses the program staff can acknowledge his excitement while using the calendar to remind him how far away this event is in a developmentally appropriate way. The compassionate staff and student relationship assists in bringing Amir back to the school-related tasks at hand, when necessary.

Anthony tells the group that he had a hard time on the bus this morning. Mrs. Tabor asks if he would like to share more, and he says no. She tells him that they can check in later about this privately if he would like. He agrees to this, and they make a plan for him to check in with Mr. Twomey after morning circle ends.

After all of the students who wished to have shared their news, they are reminded to check their individual schedules, ask a teacher if they have any questions, and move on to the next portion of their day.

Oak Program students are members of two classroom groups: the Oak classroom and their general education classroom. They often have other specialized services on their schedule as well. This means that their schedules are individualized and relatively complex. The Oak Program posts daily individual schedules for each student, posted on the wall in consistent locations (see Figure 2.1). This helps students preview and visualize their day. Students who are not yet reading have pictorial schedules to aid in their independence.

On this day, all of the students are able to do this either independently or by asking an Oak staff member for help, and then move to the

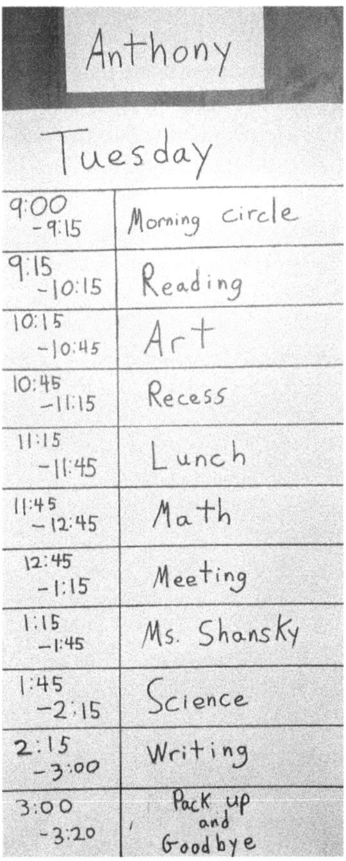

Figure 2.1 A visual schedule. Image by Michael Murray.

next part of their day. Amir walks independently to his general education classroom to begin reading instruction. Henry, along with Ms. LaChance, goes to his general education classroom for math. Anthony goes to the Oak office to check in with Mr. Twomey and will join Mrs. Tabor and Charles for their reading group when he finishes. Charles begins reading with Mrs. Tabor. Ava and Nicole begin writing services with Ms. Kelly. With a predictable, related, and secure morning, a typical day in the Oak Program has begun.

Conclusion

Morning circle is one of the two times per school day that the entire therapeutic inclusion program community gathers, the other being group therapy. This daily gathering allows the program community to connect, set the tone, and share news of the day together. Morning circle, at its core, is an act of respect oriented toward the experience of the student. What will it be helpful for them to know as we start the day? What do our students need us to know about them? The gathering of the program community as participants and audience reinforces the importance of each student's perspective and experience, and helps the program staff coordinate with the same information. Thorough previewing signals thoughtfulness and respect within the staff/student relationship, as does the dialogue prompted by the sharing of news.

Reference

Kriete, R., & Davis, C. (2014). *The morning meeting book: K-8* (3rd ed.). Center for Responsive Schools.

3 Group Psychotherapy

A Sandbox for Social Learning

A necessary element in a therapeutic process is for the person being treated to have a sense that their issues, as they see them, are being addressed. When someone is hurt, they need to feel heard. If we look at behavior as a form of communication, then our students demonstrating behavior difficulties are most keenly demonstrating that need. It can be hard to be curious about what a behavior is communicating, especially when children are acting out via difficult behaviors.

In the role of therapeutic educators, we support our students expressing themselves using speech, writing, drawing, play, role-play, and other safe methods. We want students to know they are heard and taken seriously.

Meeting is a reliable opportunity for this experience. Throughout the course of the day in the therapeutic milieu, we strive to help students feel heard and respected, but there are intrusions and limitations of various kinds given the regular flow of school demands. During meeting, everything else stops.

Meeting is group psychotherapy. While this is no secret, "group psychotherapy" is a clunky title for general use in school. "Meeting" is a much easier title for use on schedules and in conversation. For the sake of being clear about what is being described, the term "group psychotherapy" will mostly be used here.

It also must be noted that the term "group psychotherapy" can be intimidating to school staff, administrators, and even counselors depending on the nature of their previous experience and education. As this chapter will demonstrate, group psychotherapy within the therapeutic inclusion program model is a process of learning how to be in a here-and-now group (Yalom & Leszcz, 2020), while accumulating experience, understanding, social skills, and confidence, over time. Navigating speaking, listening, responsiveness, and the sharing of attention, in response to the events in and outside the therapeutic program group in the school day make up the therapeutic material. The self-disclosure of formative events that some people envision when they hear the term "group psychotherapy" is not the primary way in which the group functions.

This chapter cannot comprehensively contain a description of the known processes and principles of group psychotherapy itself. That is a topic studied and described in other volumes. Instead, this chapter on group psychotherapy highlights structure, adaptations, and aspects that are important in the

DOI: 10.4324/9781003270478-4

therapeutic inclusion programs K-12. A vignette follows developments within a student psychotherapy group, illustrating some themes of the chapter.

The case for process-oriented group psychotherapy

In a therapeutic inclusion program, much like a therapeutic school, our students have struggled with the task of managing socially within a group. The main task of the therapeutic inclusion program is for our students to learn *how to be with people*. Our students have found the experience of being in groups at school in various combinations confusing, confounding, upsetting, disturbing, and traumatizing.

While a share of therapeutic inclusion program students have experienced educational environments that most people would be able to recognize as very problematic, more often the distress is due to a mismatch between the student's needs, and what the environment provides. Because of some combination of neurological factors and their life experiences, a school that most students experience as adequately safe and supportive our students may experience as unsafe and threatening.

This leads our students toward a range of behavioral adaptations, that serve certain needs in the moment, but are ultimately maladaptive toward being in a group and learning in school. For example, students may gain a sense of security by finding various ways to demand adult attention. They may seek inappropriate control of their environment and others, in response to their anxiety. Fight, flight, and freeze responses can develop when a student feels they are under attack.

As a space and means to work with these adaptations, group psychotherapy provides us with the very basic task of coexisting and communicating during a defined period of time together. Without any distractions provided, or other activity or task keeping us busy, our student's anxieties, habits, and hopes, all have plenty of space to come to the surface. As with group psychotherapy with adults, without a sharply defined activity or task other than the expectation to be together, aspects of the group functioning that are needing attention tend to be drawn into the center.

In this way, over time and sessions, we are able to engage in a heightened conversation about the way the group functions. The term *heightened conversation* describes the different kind of conversation that is expected during group psychotherapy, with room for discussion of group dynamics, and generally of a more substantial quality than your typical lunch or recess conversation.

As the group proceeds, group and individual tendencies will inevitably be demonstrated. The heightened piece of the conversation comes as attention is brought to the habits of the group, leading toward a conversation about why we communicate the way we do, and the impact our tendencies have on the group.

This may sound lovely, but as therapists and counselors especially will know, resistance will be present in the group. Resistance is not opposition to the will of the counselor, but opposition to the possibility of change (A. Watkins, personal communication, October 2015). Therefore, ongoing discussion time must be spent on determining whether the individuals and group are interested in change. When individuals and groups express interest in change of any kind, this is the valuable purchase or foothold the counselor can use to promote self-reflection and social/emotional learning.

Group psychotherapy holds students within therapeutic relationships. These relationships exist among the group, and in relationship to the counselor and staff (Yalom & Leszcz, 2020). While sometimes it appears reasonably clear how and why a student is able to make progress on an issue within group psychotherapy, other times it is less clear. The group is a therapeutic soup made of many therapeutic factors, and the therapeutic action is not always linear or clearly observable. This will be further described in the vignette later in the chapter.

The therapeutic effect in group psychotherapy within the therapeutic inclusion program is best understood as the healthy maturation possible through relationship-based therapeutic work. Students without clinical-level social and emotional difficulties are more likely to experience this maturation within typical relationships in their school, home, and community. Through the therapeutic inclusion program, students with social, emotional, and behavioral difficulties accumulate experience with responsive, understanding, and safe adults while at school, who are specially trained and supervised in therapeutic work.

Group psychotherapy, and relationships experienced and explored within the group, are a learning ground where students learn how to be in relationship with others. Over time, the group members begin to export that understanding and confidence into other relationships.

The social sandbox

Group psychotherapy can be visualized as a social sandbox. Part of the appeal of a sandbox is that the stakes can feel relatively low. Sand castles and structures come and go. Sometimes they hold together, and sometimes they crumble. Sometimes people help each other build amazing buildings, and sometimes towers get knocked over. It is understood that these creations are temporary. It is understood that it is ok to clear it and start again.

In the sandbox, group members can play. They can safely try new building techniques. Staff can assist with the sharing of tools, encourage cooperation, and diminish occurrences like the smashing of other people's castles.

Similarly in group psychotherapy, we create a space where students can safely try new ways of being with others. They can collaborate and help each other. Program staff will encourage cooperation, student-to-student engagement, and help maintain a therapeutically productive group.

While positive support and change is fostered, the group will also experience, examine, and address difficulties and setbacks in group functioning. This can all occur within the safe boundaries of meeting. Where, like a castle in the sandbox, social learning opportunities develop, and are continually refined, restarted, and changing.

Kindergarten through eighth grade

Group psychotherapy is a venue where students share their successes, frustrations, worries, and hopes with the rest of the group. However, most of what happens in group psychotherapy with students from kindergarten to about eighth grade is especially of-the-moment. The learning is in the here-and-now and is an experiential lesson about how to be in a group. As one would expect, there is a gradual expansion toward the capacity for more prolonged and rangy discussion as students progress through grades. Between eighth and ninth grade is where a demarcation line best fits.

While adult group psychotherapy usually eschews structured turn taking, turn taking is necessary for most younger students in order to have a productive discussion. Otherwise, the group starts to feel too often chaotic and the counselor cannot maintain an adequate sense of safety for members of the group.

However, the problem of how to determine in what order we will speak is often a useful topic of discussion. A strong desire to be first is usually found among at least one or two members of any group of young children. The group is able to observe who has strong feelings about going first. We have time to hear about why it feels important to those people, and to be respectful of those feelings while discussing them.

While turn taking develops, the group can observe whether speakers demonstrate reciprocity in listening. Interruptions, distractions, and rule-testing all serve functions for the individuals and the group, and can be both observed and discussed.

However, it is not the role of the counselor to simply call out patterns and disruptive adaptations as they surface. This would generally be unproductive, and likely to make the group feel under-the-microscope.

The pathway toward helping the group develop an observational level of group and self-awareness lies within the emotional content of the group. A productive therapeutic group, at any age, will display a full range of emotion over enough time. Instead of simply highlighting unhelpful habits and adaptations, the counselor responds to the inevitable development of frustration in the group. The group frustration is an opportunity for the counselor to help the group consider whether something could possibly change. This requires the group to discuss and reflect on what is occurring within the group, and identify what could possibly change. This exercise of reflective thinking naturally leads to the group imagining various possibilities.

Ninth through 12th grade

In the high school age range, there is generally more capacity to sustain deeper discussion about the topics that students bring to the group, while still remaining connected to here-and-now concerns. These older students are also further along in the process of individuation from their families and are naturally turning toward their peers for their sense of connection, belonging, and acceptance. These elements combine to make group psychotherapy a rich opportunity for older students (W. Sharp, personal communication, November 20, 2021).

One expects a therapeutic inclusion program for students with significant social, emotional, and behavioral challenges to have members with significant delays in social and self-regulatory domains. In these upper grades, our students are also navigating an inclusion environment with adolescents who have developed toward increasingly nuanced social interactions.

A high school-aged psychotherapy group may develop the capacity for very productive conversations around long-standing individual and group issues. There is also the opportunity for significant work concerning the here-and-now. Our heightened conversation examines our interactions in the rich and evocative context of group psychotherapy occurring within our secure base, while surrounded by the large school environment.

In this age range, the group is unlikely to require structured turn taking or hand raising. The psychotherapy group becomes a special opportunity to examine the flow of less-structured interaction, creating a practice space mirroring what might occur in the cafeteria, hallway conversations, and anywhere informal groups of adolescents are gathering.

How does one know when to speak? Is it a good time to change the topic, or is it important to stay on topic right now? Does the speaker sense that the group is interested? The social exploration possibilities are limitless, and the answers to these questions lie within the group. The answers do not come from the counselor. By supporting the group in exploring these types of questions, the counselor avoids the group externalizing responsibility for group functioning and emotional content onto the counselor.

The group and group members are able to make therapeutic progress in multiple domains concurrently. One domain is regarding the actual topic being discussed. Another domain is in the development of social skills, social awareness, and self-reflection. Another domain is occurring within the emotional realm of cumulative experience being heard, listening, and being a member of the group itself.

Structural considerations

Process-oriented group psychotherapy is remarkable for a careful and strategic implementation of structure. The counselor maintains firm structure in some aspects of group functioning to promote safety, predictability, and group member agency. At the same time the counselor leaves the core activity and content of the group much less structured for the purpose of leaving space for the therapeutic needs and development of the group.

The counselor

The counselor must have experience and training in working with children and adolescents, and in group psychotherapy. Work with groups is part of any reasonable counselor education and training, and group work is common in school environments. If the counselor does not have process-oriented group psychotherapy experience, the counselor will learn through supervision with an experienced supervisor.

As well as receiving supervision, it is best practice for the counselor to be engaged in therapeutic self-care and reflection through their own individual and/or group therapy. They should have, or seek, experience attending process-oriented therapy groups. They should be engaged in a developing understanding of their own inner child and formative experiences. This will aid them in understanding and communicating with the children in the program (W. Sharp, personal communication, November 21, 2015).

Supervision

It is imperative that the group psychotherapy counselor receives quality, weekly supervision in order to discuss progress and dynamics within the program, and within group psychotherapy. Unfortunately, many school districts have allowed the therapeutic bedrock principle of supervision to fall by the wayside. This absolutely cannot be the case for the therapeutic inclusion program, and for group psychotherapy.

The program staff also has a weekly group supervision in order to discuss the ongoing program and group psychotherapy. This supervision is led by the program counselor, or by a program supervisor, depending on the individuals who make up the program staff. Supervision within the therapeutic inclusion program is further described in Chapter Ten.

Physical structure

A circle is the traditional physical structure for a psychotherapy group (Counselman, 2017) and works well with children. Staff should make an effort to intersperse with children through the circle, to promote a sense of whole group integration. While the emptiness of the center of the circle serves as a useful metaphor for how we fill the discussion-space, younger children are unmoored by the physical emptiness, exposure, and lack of anything on which to lean. A round table is useful. While maintaining physical distance during the Coronavirus pandemic, students stayed at their desks and simply rotated their chairs to face the group. This was also effective.

Group membership

Participation in meeting defines therapeutic inclusion program membership. It is the nonnegotiable element of the inclusion program member's schedule, when all members of the group will gather. This includes all therapeutic inclusion program students and staff, who make use of the therapeutic program classroom (Reinstein, 2006).

Daily group psychotherapy is ideal. However, an arrangement with group psychotherapy spaced to land on Monday, Wednesday, and Friday, with activity-based pragmatic and didactic social skills groups on Tuesdays and Thursdays has also proved effective.

It is generally best for the therapeutic inclusion classroom to operate with an open-door feel, integrated into general school functioning. Students and staff from the rest of the school should feel comfortable dropping in to say hello, or sharing space for an activity.

The exception to this is meeting. The classroom door should be closed, and there should be a sign on the door indicating that we are in meeting, as well as what time meeting will end so that students and staff outside the group can know when to come back. This practice helps define the group, brings group member's attention to the specialness of group membership, and highlights the importance of confidentiality.

Time

Thirty minutes is adequate time for recurring group psychotherapy in schools. "Start on time, end on time" is a basic concept most counselors understand in many forms of therapeutic work. However, it is not necessarily the culture of many school environments. Predictable time is important for the sense of security and empowerment of the group members. Generally in classrooms, the teacher is the master of starting and beginning. If the math teacher is in the middle of a concept they think is important, they may go a bit over. If the students are having a blast at recess on a sunny day, a teacher might extend the time. The counselor naturally finds themselves in the expected role of time master as the psychotherapy group leader.

The ability to extend or shorten time is an enormous power within a therapeutic group, where a full range of emotion is likely to be experienced. In order for the group members to feel reasonably empowered, the counselor must abdicate this power to the reliable machinations of the clock. It can be tempting to stick with a topic that the counselor feels is important, or to try to resolve something that is feeling unresolved. However, it is more important for group members to be able to count on the predictability of group beginning and ending, and not be made to feel powerless in the shadow of a time master.

As far as the student's responsibilities, it is important for them to try to be on time to the best of their ability. Sometimes teacher decisions from outside the program make it impossible for students to arrive on time, in which case students should simply do the best they can. The program co-leaders can work with their student's other teachers to help support students getting to meeting on time.

Confidentiality

Confidentiality is a large word for young children. However, the concept is simple enough, and children are reliably able to understand it and follow it. The concept is that group members will not share information learned about other group members in meeting, outside of the group. This is also made easy and clear by the seriousness with which group membership is treated, and who is allowed to be present for group psychotherapy.

Confidentiality in regard to staff and parent communication is also very different during group psychotherapy. In general, the therapeutic inclusion program should be oriented toward copious staff to parent communication about events in the school and in the therapeutic milieu. The presumption in the therapeutic inclusion program, barring unusual circumstances, is that everything that happens can be shared with parents, and much that happens is shared in the written daily communication narrative and weekly phone calls.

During group psychotherapy, this orientation is reversed. The group members are informed that this is a confidential meeting for our group. With the exception of serious safety issues, staff will not share what is discussed with parents, or others outside the group. This provides the student group members with a special space to talk about things which otherwise might feel impossible to talk about.

The counselor can further clarify that they will give parents/guardians a general sense of how meeting is going, but will not share the content of conversations without permission from the student, unless there is a serious safety concern.

This conversation also impresses upon the students how different meeting is than other parts of their school day. In practical application, group discussion is mostly of-the-moment, and these conversations are of great value to the group in negotiating how to be in a group. If something comes up that the counselor believes would be helpful to discuss with the student's parents/guardians or general education teacher, the counselor can simply ask the student if they can speak to them about it. Most often, students say yes.

Remaining in group

As with many adult psychotherapy groups, there is an expectation that group members remain seated during meeting time. Appropriate accommodations should, of course, be made to address specific needs. The starting point is to bring yourself, and only yourself, to group and be seated. Outside of specific accommodations, objects should not be brought to group psychotherapy. New groups will benefit from starting with a shorter time span to adjust to this new activity, but can generally move toward the full 30 minutes within four or five sessions.

It certainly is possible to thoughtfully integrate movement into the group, through a deliberate process in consultation with the group and the counselor's supervisor. However, managing the task of simply sharing the conversational space in a therapeutic and productive manner is generally enough to keep the group and the group leaders fully occupied. Group psychotherapy is primarily a talk therapy, and the full therapeutic inclusion program and milieu offers a range of therapies including those that are not primarily language-based.

Respect

This is a simple expectation that is reviewed in almost any classroom—be respectful of others and yourself. This encompasses a large range of possibilities in individual and group behavior. Students in grades kindergarten, first, and even into second grade often do not have an adequate understanding of what respect encompasses. When going over rules of meeting, explicit instruction is necessary. For example, that we will not use insults or taunting names in the group. This helps students be better prepared to meet similar expectations in other environments, including their general education classrooms. Also, the importance of honesty should be emphasized. While members do not have to share any particular thing, the things they choose to share should be honest.

Behavior management

As described later in the chapter, the counselor and staff use thoughtful judgment to provide the group with a carefully calibrated, "just right" opportunity for self-management. There are social and behavioral domains to consider and monitor regarding the group's capacity for self-management, and these realms overlap. Moreover, there is a wide range across groups of relative strengths and weaknesses in these domains. Just as it is not unusual for a group to have deficits in social and behavioral domains, it is also not unusual for a given group to be strong in one domain, but not the other.

The therapeutic inclusion program is relationship-based, and group psychotherapy provides a place for the group to more deeply understand the relationships that hold their school experience. As described in Chapter Seven, the program uses some behaviorist strategies, always within the context of the safe and authentic care relationship. This includes behavior intervention plans, and program-specific behavior response plans to promote positive growth and maintain a safe and predictable-enough environment in the therapeutic inclusion program. For some groups, these specialized program plans can be set aside during group psychotherapy. This can again signal to students that we are engaged in a different kind of activity together.

Some groups will not maintain an atmosphere safe-enough for therapeutic work without staff maintaining program behavioral plans and responses. It is up to the program counselor and program staff to determine and monitor what will work for the group, calibrated toward the group practicing self-management with a degree of responsibility that they can reasonably handle.

Group preparation

Introducing group psychotherapy

The first two sessions are called "About Meeting" and can be devoted to introducing meeting (group psychotherapy) to new group members, as well as reviewing it for returning members. It is very important to structure these fundamentally informational sessions very differently than group psychotherapy itself. In order to clearly differentiate these introductions from group psychotherapy, they should look and feel more like a traditional school lesson.

During these introductory lessons, the counselor is an expert and there is the work of disseminating information about group psychotherapy to the group. It needs to be clear to the group that these lessons are not group psychotherapy. Group members should be informed about how the seats will be arranged for group psychotherapy, that only members of the group will be in the room, and that when we are in meeting there will be a sign on the door asking visitors to return later. When the time comes for the first group psychotherapy session, the group members should experience that it is distinctly different from a school lesson, or the introduction group psychotherapy sessions.

The counselor's introduction to group psychotherapy will be tailored to their unique group, and their developmental levels. In the first About Meeting session, the counselor may want to share some of the following: The purpose of the group is practicing *how to be with people.* The counselor could include that for members of the program, it has been hard sometimes to be in groups. In group psychotherapy, we will practice being in a group. Members will have an opportunity to learn more about themselves. Group members can learn about what it is like for other people to be with them.

While introducing group psychotherapy, the counselor can share that what students learn about *how to be with people* in this group could be helpful to them in other settings with friends, classmates, and family members. The counselor can also include that while the group may talk about a whole range of things, the group will often return to the "here and now" of how the group is doing.

It is important that group members agree to follow these three basic principles in order to participate: (1) Be on time (to the best of your ability), (2) Confidentiality, and (3) Respect.

Individual meeting goals

The second About Meeting session reviews information from session one and then focuses on individual meeting goals. Every group member, both students and staff, should choose a personal goal to work on in meeting (A. Watkins, personal communication, October 2015). Each individual will be provided with a developmentally appropriate form to write their goal (see Figure 3.1). For younger students "My goal is" may be provided for them as a sentence starter. However, this is not a writing exercise and any handwriting assistance that is necessary or helpful should be provided. An individual meeting goal should be something that can be reasonably worked on in group psychotherapy, as well as something the students are comfortable with other members of the group being aware of. If necessary, examples can be provided.

The following are goals that students have developed:

> "My goal for meeting this year is to help the Oak Program have fun."
>
> "My goal for meeting this year is to be nice, kind, and listen."

Figure 3.1 Meeting goal template. Image by Michael Murray.

> "My goal for meeting this year is to make it easier for people to understand me better."
>
> "My goal for meeting this year is to become ruler of the galaxy."
>
> Unexpected goals like the last one can also provide plenty to work with in the group!

It is important for students to know, in order to ease any sense of pressure, that they are not committing to a goal for the rest of the year. It will be okay to change their mind about their goal when they want. For the counselor, following the progression of a group member's changing goal provides excellent discussion material, and can help group members feel attended to and respected.

Staff member goals are different. They exist in order to reflect the reality that we are all working on things. At the same time, it should be clear that the purpose of the group is to serve the diverse needs of the students. Therefore, staff goals should be bounded within their roles as therapeutic educators. For example, in a year impacted by unpredictable school arrangements demanded by COVID, a counselor goal was "My goal for meeting this year is to help create an adaptable meeting."

All program staff members attend group psychotherapy. New staff are unlikely to have previous experience with group psychotherapy. Staff members can support the group, following the lead of the counselor. They learn about group psychotherapy by attending the groups and through discussions at weekly supervision.

Other examples of staff member meeting goals include:

> "My goal for meeting this year is to help make a safe space for kids to talk about what they're thinking and feeling."
>
> "My goal for meeting this year is to help children have more fun at meeting."

The student goals are very helpful for group discussion material. Bringing the self-generated individual goals into the conversation periodically helps students feel respected and supports a cohesive sense of narrative for the group. It is important that when bringing up goals that the counselor remains nonjudgmental. This leaves the group member open to comment on any sense of progress toward their goal, or how they feel about their goal at this particular point in time.

A counselor's attuned and nonjudgmental approach to discussing personal goals will encourage group members to feel ownership of their progress.

Group members may feel proud of progress, or frustrated by lack of progress. They may dismiss their goals, or change their goals. If group members change their goals, they do not need to write down the new one. The counselor should track goal changes and return to the discussion periodically. The counselor can help hold a narrative arc of group member's relationships with their goals. Going over this narrative in the group, devoid of counselor value judgments, helps the group member experience feeling held-in-mind by the counselor and group.

The counselor's multiple roles

The program counselor works within the therapeutic program classroom, assists in classes, and is likely to do some teaching with the support of the special education teacher. The program counselor also manages much of the parent communication. This, as well as leading group psychotherapy, creates a multiplicity of roles for the counselor. In traditional group psychotherapy, a key feature is that the group leader does not otherwise have a role in the group member's lives. Regardless of whether or not this would be advantageous in the program setting, this is generally not the case in the therapeutic inclusion program.

Therefore, in order to cultivate a welcoming and safe group despite the presence of the staff's multiple roles, the counselor must establish a different atmosphere during group psychotherapy. For example, the students should know that what they share during group psychotherapy will never be deployed in an antagonistic way against them outside of group psychotherapy. It is usually helpful to articulate this clearly to the group.

For example, a student might share during group psychotherapy that they would like to stop disrupting morning circle. The following morning circle, the student acts out disruptively. The counselor, or any staff member, must not say anything like "you said in meeting that you wanted to stop that." Perhaps, the student or counselor might return to the topic during the next group psychotherapy session.

In the therapeutic inclusion program the dynamics of rules, adult authority, and students who struggle with behavior will sometimes lead to inevitable student feelings of "getting in trouble," when staff must reinforce limits. In group psychotherapy, there is an effort to establish a different dynamic among the same group of people. Limit testing and boundary crossing from other parts of the day can be discussed with a focus firmly on the experience of the student.

If the student develops trust that the counselor and staff is truly interested in their experience, and that the staff is not in effect seeking information to gain advantage in struggles over limit testing, this is possible.

Other times, the counselor might notice that elements of the conversation from group psychotherapy might be useful to the student outside of group psychotherapy. For example, during group psychotherapy a student and staff member come up with a hand signal to use to signal for a break during general education classes. Or, the student might appreciate a reminder outside group psychotherapy around a particular issue on which they are working. In these cases, the counselor should be explicit and confirm the plan with the student.

The entire therapeutic inclusion program staff participates in group psychotherapy, and must contend with the same concerns as the counselor around inhabiting multiple roles. In most cases, the counselor is in a position to model this while co-leading the group with their program co-leader, the special education teacher.

Learning pragmatic social skills in group psychotherapy

Didactic, pragmatic social skills curriculums such as Social Thinking® are excellent for many children. Students in the therapeutic inclusion program should have exposure to these stories, lessons, and activity-based curricula, because many students find them very helpful.

The social skills learning that happens in group psychotherapy is not in competition with didactic social skills lessons. The two approaches can be very effective in parallel. Additionally, some students are highly resistant to didactic social skills lessons. Others may have had a period where they gained from lessons and have reached a stage where they intellectually know the lessons but are having difficulty applying them.

The heightened conversation during group psychotherapy allows for students to experience and understand more about the hows and whys of social skills. Social skills are ultimately about being understood, understanding others, and helping people feel comfortable with you. In group psychotherapy, we can richly explore these themes. It is a bit like having a magic freeze button, where we can stop and explore what is happening with the group and individuals. Except, these discussions become normalized within the psychotherapy group, making the dramatic freeze unnecessary.

Developing social skills helps a group maintain a thoughtful sense of flow and discussion. As teachers of very young students know, younger students usually need significant structure from adults in order to maintain on-topic and productive discussions. In terms of social skills, the group psychotherapy counselor's role is to support the group in practicing skills by allowing them to manage as much of the group discussion and group functioning as they can. This requires some calibrative judgment on the counselor's part.

It is similar to reading teachers striving to provide collections of books to those learning to read that are at the "just right" level. For the "just right" reading approach there should be some easier books in the bunch, there should be some more challenging ones, but all in all not too easy and not too hard. The group psychotherapy counselor in the therapeutic inclusion program must strive to allow the group to operate similarly in terms of social skills and group functioning.

A practical application of this concept can be described through discussing how to support turn taking in the group. A high school group may need relatively little guidance to ensure that members feel that they are getting an adequate and fair-enough opportunity to contribute to the group. Younger students, such as kindergarten through third grade, will likely need significant support.

The younger age range of students will likely need explicit turn taking. They might require an object that is passed to make tactile and observable whose turn it is. The object will signify who is currently leading the conversation, as well as who the conversation is currently organized around. To help students have an adequate sense of structure, a "good part, hard part" format is useful (D. Reinstein, personal communication, 2002). This structure provides that members should take a turn and share something that is going well, and something that is difficult.

Among younger students, hand raising is likely necessary. However, rather than have an adult call on members who have raised their hand, this can usually be managed by the student who is taking a turn. This is an example of providing a group a just right level of self-management.

Over time, there is room for social skills development. Hand raising, in a small group, shifts the responsibility for figuring out when to speak from each individual, toward one group manager. Can the members of the group figure out when the right time to speak is on their own? Since hand raising is ultimately some extra work, groups naturally forget to do it at times. When the counselor notices the group has forgotten to hand-raise but is managing a reasonable flow and timing of conversation, this is good material for discussion.

The opportunities to address social skills in this method are endless. The method also offers the distinct advantage that the social skills issues that need attention naturally present themselves. While any number of social skills topics could be addressed in group psychotherapy, some popular themes include listening, not interrupting, staying on topic, empathizing, and leaving space for others to speak.

The following vignette demonstrates the therapeutic effect of accumulating experience over time in group psychotherapy, along with some of the interventions and changes experienced.

The Oak group

The Oak group was a largely consistent group of students and staff over two school years, who ranged from six to nine years old at the outset. The group began the school year with four students, and four program staff members. By October the group expanded to five students. They met for group psychotherapy on Mondays, Wednesday, and Fridays, for 30 minutes each session.

The Oak group initially sat around a circular table and used an egg-shaped piece of carved wood as a talking object. A good part/hard part format was established, where students were expected to share something that was going well and something that was difficult at each meeting. The students were encouraged to choose topics for sharing that were topical to the day, and close to the here-and-now. Otherwise, children have a tendency to find repetitive shares, as an understandable way to avoid the work of considering what is happening for them in the here-and-now.

First graders Amir and Nicole were in the group. Amir was a creative and fun group member. He had an idiosyncratic perspective, concurrent with his idiosyncratic use of language. These qualities would often make it difficult for others to understand his stories, across settings. He had significant social, emotional, and self-regulation delays. He could be extremely rigid, and had frequent and intense tantrums. He was diagnosed through the school system with developmental delay.

Nicole was a socially motivated and endearing group member. She had significant emotional regulation difficulties, engaged in prolonged struggle-seeking, and explosive tantrums. Nicole also carried a diagnosis of developmental delay, which encompassed learning disabilities.

The group's second graders were Anthony and Henry. Anthony was an emotionally tuned-in and thoughtful member of the Oak group. Anthony had wide emotional lability, as well as difficulty with self-regulation. His low mood dips would often correspond with a reflexively antagonistic orientation toward school staff, and explosive struggles, sometimes with significant physical aggression. He also had a pronounced reading disability. He was diagnosed through the school system with developmental delay and a specific learning disability in reading.

Henry was a clever and sensitive group member, with extremely low impulse control. He was incredibly prolific in his rule and safety testing, which would often occur continuously throughout a school day. Henry was diagnosed with ADHD and generalized anxiety disorder.

The oldest member of the Oak group was Aida, in third grade. Aida was a talented artist and capable student, who struggled with social understanding and functioning, and rigidity. She was diagnosed with autism.

Beginnings and obstacles

For some students, the distinctly different feel of group psychotherapy brings out a different kind of personal presentation. Other students are more or less consistent across settings at school. Either way, in this case, the issues that were needing attention for the group and individuals came to the fore quickly.

Amir, who was already difficult to understand, shared his most outlandish and confusing stories during group psychotherapy. It was not at all clear whether he was following the group agreement to be honest. Perhaps the challenge he presented to the group in determining what is real and what is not was in fact the same challenge he was experiencing himself. This came to a head in Amir's insistence that his father *is* Link, from the legendary Zelda® video game series. Amir's conviction on this point was unshakeable, which forced group members to consider accepting that Amir believes this to be true, even when they understood that Amir's attestation was not possible.

Nicole could make helpful contributions to the group process, but also had a consistent tendency to stir up conflict with other group members, which would introduce significant distress to the group. There's a colloquial British term for her style of introducing conflict, "winding up." Nicole would do the winding through comments and interruptions, and it was usually some other group member who would lose their composure and have an outburst. Observing Nicole, this presented as a relational habit playing out with low self-awareness.

This pattern, of Nicole winding up another group member and the other group member acting out, began to take up significant space in group psychotherapy. It was negatively and seriously impacting the group-sense of whether meeting could be a useful and safe-enough place to share and grow toward health. Mr. Twomey, the program therapist, felt that in order to reasonably moderate the degree of distress experienced in the group and cultivate a group that could operate therapeutically, this winding-up had to be worked on directly. During group psychotherapy Mr. Twomey explained to Nicole how it is possible to wind-up other people then watch them go, just like a wind-up toy. He brought in a little plastic robot wind-up toy from home to demonstrate how it works. Mr. Twomey talked about how it could feel good and powerful for the winder, and he also discussed the distress it causes. This description was heard by Nicole and the group. The demonstration built group awareness, reducing future group reactivity to Nicole's winding-up tendency. Nicole wanted to be kind. However, this impulse, partly due to the rewarding sense of control that it brought, was a hard tendency to stop. After discussing it explicitly, Mr. Twomey did his best to bring winding-up to her attention as soon as it started, which allowed them to work on it together.

This conversation did not cause a sudden transformation by any means. However, this conversation, and others like it, do lay the groundwork for incremental positive change. While direct interventions from the leader are likely to be a part of the therapeutic process, they are not one of the primary therapeutic factors in the psychotherapy group. The primary therapeutic factors are best understood as the accumulation of positive group experience and social skill within a cohesive and related group. Within Yalom and Leszcz's 11 therapeutic factors, "imparting information" is but one of them, and is not specific to information coming from the counselor. Their other 10 therapeutic factors are interdependent with the group process (Yalom & Leszcz, 2020). Mr. Twomey's intervention with Nicole was done with the primary intention of preserving an environment where the other therapeutic factors would continue to be able to have positive effect on the group.

Anthony, who had very significant emotional regulation difficulties which were complicated by a highly fluctuating mood, was at the same time unusually skilled in emotional and social understanding. Sometimes, in a low mood, he would shut down during meeting. But otherwise, he was able to demonstrate and exercise his significant empathic understanding of others. His empathic sensitivity resulted in a tendency to sacrifice attention to himself and conversational space in the group, so that other group member's needs and demands could be met. Part of the group work was exploring Anthony's deservedness of attention and time during group psychotherapy, even when others were more outwardly demanding.

Henry's presentation during meeting was in line with his general presentation, featuring copious limit testing. Henry was also highly defended around conversations containing emotional content. The primary work of group psychotherapy for Henry was accumulating positive experience functioning as a member of a group. This experience could be accumulated through his efforts, with significant support from program staff.

The Oak group's oldest student Aida, doing so very well in the milieu and in her general education classes, presented with serious difficulty during group psychotherapy. She would express her distress by repeatedly and dramatically moving her chair back from the group. Aida would do this with an affect combining elements of enjoyable mischief and anger. As the oldest and the tallest student, the impact her behavior had on the other students was significant. It signaled to the others that the structure was not holding. Other group members would follow suit with behaviors that highlighted the loss of structure. They made random noises and gestures. The group engaged in a performance of silly chaos that approached parody. The exception was Anthony, who would wait out the chaos in quiet exasperation.

Group psychotherapy requires group leaders to hold multiple and sometimes conflicting truths simultaneously. This applies not just to the perspectives of the group members, but also regarding how to best foster a therapeutic group. For example, the structure of group psychotherapy should be kept as simple as reasonably possible in order to help students feel empowered. This allows for personal change, and leaves room for the emergence of the issues that need attention, which otherwise might remain beyond what we can perceive. At the same time, Aida's continued behavior amounted to the pulling of a weight-bearing pin in the structure. We tried various responses within the established group structure, including various approaches of discussion, and shifting our attention to other needs in the group. But our efforts were not successful in resolving Aida's behavior, and its impact on the group.

Mrs. Tabor, Oak Program co-leader and special education teacher, suggested that if Aida made it through group psychotherapy without pushing her chair back from the group, she could be rewarded with extra painting time after the group. On the face of it, this was an undesirable intervention for group psychotherapy, being student behavior intervention to meet a goal desired by program staff. But, Aida's presentation during group psychotherapy was making it impossible for the group to function therapeutically, and this was going on over many sessions with no end in sight. The painting reward intervention was implemented, and Aida responded well, allowing the group to return to therapeutic functioning.

This supported the Oak group returning to their "just right" social and therapeutic level. Room and flexibility in the structure is necessary to allow for the sense of things getting off track, or at times to not be going well. It is often these times when we learn about the issues that need attention and work. These circumstances present the group with the opportunity for change that comes from the whole group, not simply from the staff. Staff imposed adjustments are less likely to bring about deeper internal change in the students. However, there is nothing therapeutic or kind about presenting a group with a task that they are demonstrating is well beyond their ability to perform.

An established group at work

Within Bruce Tuckman's group development model (forming, storming, norming, performing, and adjourning) resolving this challenge in order to move to group functioning marked the end of the group's initial storming phase (1965). By this stage, toward the end of November in the group's first year, they were establishing norms of functioning. The group was busy with here-and-now concerns such as what order we will go in for sharing, and whether we want to both be listened to, *and* to listen. While we worked on these ways of being together, the students gained much needed experience being held and valued within a responsive and attuned group.

The Oak group continued this way, accumulating experience, confidence, and knowledge while encountering ups and downs, and maturing through the school year. As the end of the school year neared, meeting took on importance as a place of consistency amidst approaching change.

And change arrived: Over the summer, Aida's family moved overseas. Nicole and Amir moved up to second grade, while Anthony and Henry moved up to third grade. The four remaining students continued in the Oak Program.

As their second year began, the remaining students recognized the goodbye to Aida, while maintaining a mostly consistent group. Given the accumulated experience and some maturity, Mr. Twomey found that students were able to keep track of whose turn it was to speak without a talking object. As time progressed, hand raising was often not needed. The group and individuals were growing in their responsibility for determining when to speak.

In the new school year, Amir had left his seemingly fantastical stories behind and had become much easier to understand. Nicole continued to aim for kindness and continued to need support to develop self-awareness and new ways of being with others. Anthony demonstrated a deepening emotional intelligence and emerged as a more active empathic leader in the group. His growth in group psychotherapy corresponded with tremendous progress in his self-regulation abilities globally.

Henry's presentation was variable. He often relied on a rewarding behavior intervention system, and the reminders of staff in order to maintain himself throughout the day, including group psychotherapy. He also became perhaps even more consistent in his deep resistance toward using his time in group psychotherapy to engage in material that appeared to be of actual importance to himself. Henry's approach was minimal and disengaged, with a performative edge that gave the impression he was making a point with his disengagement. The meaning of the message he was sending was explored, but the explorations were not particularly productive.

However, both Henry and Mr. Twomey separately discussed the general sense of how meeting was going with his mother. During one weekly phone conversation, Henry's mother suggested to Mr. Twomey that he would like to tell a joke during group psychotherapy. This sounded delightful to Mr. Twomey, and he talked to Henry about it. At the next meeting Henry told a good joke he learned from a joke book (What does Batman like in his drink? Just Ice.) The group really enjoyed his joke and wanted to tell their own. It became a tradition (though not a rule) that students might share a joke at the end of their turn. The jokes were improvised, in the form of questions, and generally inscrutable. Students greatly enjoyed the ritual of each guessing the possible punch line. These developments opened the door for Henry to begin to engage with meeting again, and he became more meaningfully and explicitly involved. Perhaps he felt validated to see his ability to meaningfully influence the group, or that the mutual communication and connection to his mother allowed change to feel sufficiently safe.

The group was joined near the end of this time period by a second-grade student named Ava. Previous to joining the therapeutic inclusion program Ava appeared depressed, was doing almost no school work, and having explosive behavioral episodes. With careful previewing and a gradual process Ava was able to join the group, and the established group accepted and included her.

This group of students with significant social, emotional, and behavioral difficulties matured significantly over this period in group psychotherapy. They developed through a challenging storming phase which called for unconventional interventions, said goodbye to a member, grew in their capacity to self-manage socially and in group function, made progress in their individual areas of need, and welcomed a new member. Throughout, group psychotherapy served as an important shared experience of being with people and belonging, and a venue for important group discussions pertaining to the functioning of the therapeutic inclusion program group.

Conclusion

One aspect of group psychotherapy with children and adolescents that differentiates the experience from an adult group is that the group will inevitably mature. The group development is powered by the engines of the individual member's development of skills, knowledge, physical development, and cognitive ability. Long-term group psychotherapy can serve as a helpful influence on the trajectory of the student's natural development. The ongoing maturation process of children and adolescents is a great benefit to the work of group psychotherapy.

The accumulation of time and experience in a group, in tandem with the heightened conversation, leads to deeper self and social understandings, as well as social skill and confidence about being a member of a group.

The psychotherapy group member's confidence, knowledge, and skill is generalized to other groups. They carry these into their general education classrooms, the cafeteria and recess, as well as back home to their families, and other environments.

When lay people think of group psychotherapy, they may envision deeply personal sharing and self-disclosure in a group format. However, the therapeutic factors at work are not dependent on self-disclosure. The present and openly available goings-on of the group provide more than enough material to work with therapeutically. This may include discussions of our routines, the quality of listening in the group, group members helping other members understand an experience, or the events of today's recess. The open and available possibilities are endless.

It is naturally the aim of the counselor to create a psychotherapy group where students can feel safe and secure with disclosing thoughts, feelings, and events that may otherwise feel too difficult to share (Schectman, 2007). This does occur and can be an important part of a therapeutic process. However, it is important for the staff to understand that group self-disclosure is not mandated by the therapeutic process and is not the primary way the therapeutic process develops in the therapeutic inclusion program.

A vignette can only capture a glimmer of what occurs in a long-term student psychotherapy group. The vignette in this chapter highlights the aspects that were most therapeutic for the Oak group. These were the accumulation of experience, confidence, skills, and understanding over time, along with interventions to preserve group cohesion and hope.

References

Counselman, E. F. (2017). First you put your chairs in a circle: Becoming a group therapist. *International Journal of Group Psychotherapy*, 67(1), 124–133.

Reinstein, D. K. (2006). *To hold and be held: The therapeutic school as a holding environment.* Routledge.

Schectman, Z. (2007). *Group counseling and psychotherapy with children and adolescents: Theory, Research, and Practice.* Routledge.

Tuckman, B. W. (1965). Developmental sequence in small groups. *Psychological Bulletin*, 63(6), 384–399.

Yalom, I. D., & Leszcz, M. (2020). *The theory and practice of group psychotherapy* (6th ed.). Basic Books.

4 Into the General Education Environment

This chapter describes the therapeutic inclusion program's approach to collaboration with general education colleagues in the general education environment. Maintaining access to the social and academic resources of the general education setting is the primary reason why therapeutic inclusion is preferable to substantially separate or out-of-district placements, whenever appropriate. Increasingly, school districts have attempted to cobble together programs. Where programs do exist, most school districts do not offer a program as effective as this model. Poorly conceived and maintained programs lead to ongoing frustration, contentious relationships with parents/guardians, high staff turnover, and out-of-district placements.

This chapter describes an approach toward professional collaboration rooted in the relationship-based model, in parallel process to the relationship-based therapeutic experience of the student. The program supports general education teachers and their education goals and uses weekly meetings to form and maintain working relationships. Approaches to social and academic integration and support are outlined and explained. Woven throughout the chapter are the stories of Ansh, Paul, and their teachers, bringing the therapeutic inclusion program's functioning into sharper focus.

"Inclusion" includes students with social, emotional, and behavioral difficulties

The therapeutic inclusion program carries the significant benefit of including our students with social, emotional, and behavioral difficulties with their peers to the maximum extent possible. Inclusion is best practice, a reality reflected in the educational discourse for over 30 years (Pearpoint et al., 1992). Furthermore, inclusion is supported by the law through the federal Individuals with Disabilities Education Act which was passed in 1975 (originally as the Education for All Handicapped Children Act), requiring that students are educated within the least restrictive environment (LRE). LRE begins with the general education environment and stipulates that students with disabilities must be placed alongside their nondisabled peers, unless, even with support and services, an education cannot be provided in the general education environment (Individuals with Disabilities Education Act, 2004).

DOI: 10.4324/9781003270478-5

The development of inclusion practices has made less restrictive environments available to an increasingly diverse range of students. The therapeutic inclusion program adds to a growing tradition of innovations that have expanded inclusion in general education classrooms. The theory of inclusive practice recognizes that all students benefit from meaningful, challenging curriculum delivered in the general education classroom via differentiated instruction that reaches the needs of all learners (Salend, 2007). Students with emotional disabilities may exhibit impulsivity, low frustration tolerance, low self-esteem, delayed social skills, and increased off-task behavior (Allen & Cowdery, 2012). As a result, these students run a greater risk of performing poorly in all academic areas, in addition to the risk of not being accepted in their school communities by both their peers and teachers.

Salend (2007) notes that there is a lower rate of placement in inclusion environments for students with emotional and behavior disorders when compared to other students with high-incidence disabilities (p. 72). Therapeutic inclusion programming aims to remedy this injustice. When students receive a portion of their special education services within their school-based therapeutic milieu, they can spend a significant amount of time in the general education environment. Social and academic opportunities not available in a substantially separate environment become available to our therapeutic inclusion program students.

A story of two third-graders

Ansh

Ansh is a third-grade student who presents with anxiety and ADHD. Ansh attended his neighborhood school beginning in kindergarten with an individualized education program. Ansh had difficulty attending to the curriculum in the classroom and, beginning in first grade, was not making effective progress academically. Additionally, Ansh had difficulty sitting in the classroom and often moved around the room, called out, and distracted other students, which his teachers had difficulty managing.

As first grade continued Ansh began to develop a very poor view of himself as a student and a learner, and this self-image only deepened in second grade. Though testing indicated that Ansh had average cognitive abilities, his disabilities made it extremely difficult to access the curriculum in the general education environment without significant accommodations. Ansh's view of himself as a learner led him to believe that school was simply not for him. His attempts to present his best effort at school stopped. Feeling that academic success was not possible, Ansh tried to salvage social success through inappropriate humor, disrupting the classroom, and presenting an attitude of not caring. Ansh would engage in arguments and struggles with his teacher, who would then call the assistant principal. Ansh would be removed from the classroom, and he would have a conversation with the assistant principal about what had happened that day. These conversations never dug to the root of Ansh's perceived school failure.

Ansh's inability to make effective progress in the curriculum, paired with his disruptive behavior in the classroom, and the school's inability to manage his behavior, led his parents to request an outplacement to a private school. His parents felt a private therapeutic school could better meet Ansh's needs given his disabilities and current presentation. Ansh's school system ultimately recognized that they did not have a sufficient social–emotional learning program to meet his needs. Beginning in third grade, Ansh began at a private therapeutic school for students with behavioral and emotional difficulties. An overview of his day is presented below.

Ansh's morning

Ansh wakes up at 5:30 am as he has to be ready for door-to-door van transportation to his school, which is 45 minutes away. Ansh is able to ride the van easily, in contrast to the 15-minute school bus ride that he previously took to his neighborhood school that was full of angst and chaos. Ansh sits in the van listening to music on his headphones for 30 minutes, then picks up one other student along the way. Ansh does not engage with the other student, who is in the sixth grade, on the van.

When they arrive at school, a staff member comes out to greet Ansh and take him off of the van. Ansh goes into his classroom with his teacher and six other students, with whom Ansh will spend the majority of the remainder of the day. Ansh receives all of his academic instruction in this classroom. Some of his classmates present similarly to Ansh, others have a range of behavioral challenges including acting out aggressively in the school environment. These behaviors are well managed at Ansh's school. They are not out of the ordinary and the staff and teachers there know how to work with students with behavioral outbursts and emotional dysregulation. Ansh feels safe in his new school and better understood. His teachers are working with him to develop an understanding of himself as a learner in an alternate environment with students who present with similar challenges.

Paul

Paul is a third-grade student who has recently outgrown the disability diagnosis of developmental delay and has been diagnosed with generalized anxiety disorder through a neuropsychological evaluation that his parents paid for privately outside of school. Paul has attended his neighborhood school since kindergarten where he has presented with difficulty integrating into his general education classroom due to behavioral outbursts and conflicts with peers. Paul's school has a therapeutic inclusion program embedded within their special education programming. Paul has been a member of his school's therapeutic inclusion program since his first-grade year.

Paul's morning

Paul arrives at school in the morning in a van, along with one other student from the school who has medical needs which require specialized transportation. Many of Paul's classmates in the Oak program arrive on the school bus, but the environment is loud, chaotic, unstructured, and unsupervised. The bus environment was overwhelming for Paul. Currently his day begins with a short, quiet van ride to school. When Paul arrives at school an Oak paraprofessional, Ms. LaChance, greets him and the other student in the van. Paul looks to be in good spirits and walks to his classroom alone. Ms. LaChance says that she will meet him down there in a few minutes.

Paul begins to walk to his general education classroom and sees a peer along the way. He runs to say hello and they walk down the hall, happy to be together and talking about Pokemon, a shared interest. When Paul arrives in the classroom he and his classmate are greeted by their teacher, Mrs. Chen. His friend begins his morning routine, hanging up his coat and backpack, and Paul follows suit.

At this point, Ms. LaChance has made her way to Paul's general education classroom and quietly reminds him that it's time to go to the Oak room for morning circle. Paul leaves his general education classroom to begin his day with the typical structure and routine of his therapeutic milieu, though he will be back shortly to begin academic instruction with his peers in his third-grade classroom.

Both Paul and Ansh have had a successful morning, and are off to start what is hopefully a happy and productive school day. However, their days will look quite different from one another. Even from the short description of these two boys' mornings, one can see that there are significant opportunities that can be afforded to students when they are given time, space, and support to be with their peers. Being an integral part of a diverse classroom community is hugely important to the school experience. It's an experience that every student deserves to have.

If students are not provided with the correct and proper amount of support, it can be easy for a student with significant social/emotional or behavioral difficulties to feel separate from their peers and isolated from the community even while attending their public school. When inclusion is implemented well, the general education environment provides rich academic and social opportunities.

Social opportunities

In order to become a well-rounded person, and contributing and functional member of society, it is necessary to develop social skills. Developing the skills to communicate with the world begins at a very young age, and continue to be honed and developed throughout one's adolescence and adulthood. The school environment is one of the primary settings where this work occurs.

School provides both structured and unstructured blocks of time for students to interact with one another. A public school environment provides a mix of students, both neurotypical and neurodivergent, that mirrors the outside world. This is an invaluable opportunity for social learning and growth to occur, for all students to learn how to be around one another. (We must note that the dichotomy between neurotypical and neurodivergent is a major oversimplification, but we use it to reflect how schools classify students when qualifying for special education services.)

In addition to social opportunities provided via formal instructional learning that occurs in the classroom environment, there are a variety of times throughout the school day that are available for students to be social with their peers such as snack, recess, and lunch. During these times, students with social and emotional difficulties can struggle significantly if not provided with adequate support as this time is largely unstructured and minimally supervised. These struggles can range from anxiety in students to verbal or physical altercations with peers.

The therapeutic inclusion program supports the program staff in knowing each student closely, and providing a responsive level of support. There will be students in the program who can successfully access less structured school periods, such as lunch and recess, with minimal or no support. Other students will need support during a portion of these unstructured times. Some benefit from having a therapeutic inclusion program staff member present, and some students may require staff to be constantly within earshot. With adequate support, students who previously had significant difficulties with these unstructured times can utilize the social coaching and supervision of the therapeutic inclusion staff in order to begin to have successful play and social times with their peers.

Paul, given his impulsivity and proclivity to utilize inappropriate language and topics to gain attention, requires consistent supervision from therapeutic inclusion staff during all unstructured times of the day. The staff provides this supervision in a manner mindful of the social impact of the supervision itself. This is best done by the program staff integrating into the classroom at large, being responsive to Paul and the group's dynamics. While calibrating this support can be challenging, the staff presence is less stigmatizing for Paul than frequent verbal altercations with his peers.

Social opportunities embedded within academics

The ability for Paul to successfully access peer relationships throughout the day is made possible by his membership in the milieu of the therapeutic inclusion program. Paul is able to have a secure home base, knowing that should a social setback occur or an emotional outburst bubble to the surface, there is a safe place to have and process those feelings. He can do so with a trusted and skilled adult.

Without this, Paul's membership in his general education classroom would be too overwhelming. The general education environment can be overstimulating due to the sheer number of people, noise level, and activity that occurs in a classroom every day. Additionally, most classrooms do not maintain a level of consistency optimally calibrated for students with social and emotional difficulties. Children can be unpredictable and classroom teachers don't always provide the amount of previewing and consistent response that is necessary for students with significant social, emotional, and behavioral needs to be successful. In such an environment, the likelihood of something unexpected or difficult occurring is quite probable. However, Paul's membership in the Oak Program allows him to feel secure enough in his school environment, enabling him to benefit from the general education classroom for a large portion of his day.

After Paul has completed his morning routine in Mrs. Chen's room, he heads down to the Oak classroom for morning circle. As described in Chapter Two, morning circle allows for a consistent routine for Paul. Additionally, Paul's day is previewed in detail, so that he knows exactly what to expect. He is able to ask any questions that he needs to and fill in his teachers on anything that feels important to him that day. Morning circle lasts only about 15 minutes, yet it is a critical and anchoring piece of the day for Paul, and the other members of the Oak community.

After morning circle is complete, Paul walks down to his third-grade class to begin his reading instruction for the day. At times, Paul likes to walk independently to his classrooms. Other days he likes to walk with an Oak staff member and talk about anything ranging from a superhero movie, to a difficult night at home, to his plan for recess that day.

With the right support in place, Paul is able to access all of the general education curricula in third grade. His presentation varies from day to day, and there are some days where an Oak staff member will deliver his academic instruction in the therapeutic inclusion classroom. Today, like most days, Paul is equipped to receive his reading lesson in the general education classroom. The teacher begins with phonics instruction, where Paul is able to follow along with an occasional reminder from his special education teacher, Mrs. Tabor. Mrs. Tabor also spends her time aiding other students in the classroom who benefit from some support with the lesson.

During phonics, the class is instructed to write a sentence with a target word, which Paul does swiftly. Mrs. Chen then asks for volunteers to read their sentences aloud. Paul raises his hand quickly and quietly, and Mrs. Tabor casually passes by his desk to look at this sentence. His sentence is inappropriate for the third-grade classroom environment. With the practice word being *target*, Paul has written "I shot a machine gun at the target." The Oak teacher gives a hand signal to Mrs. Chen, cueing her not to call on Paul this time, and bends down to speak with Paul about his sentence. Paul, who is aware that his work was not appropriate for the classroom, erases it and writes another sentence before moving on. These routines, which have been honed through a partnership with Mrs. Chen, allow Paul to be successful in the classroom. He, of course, still has impulses to gain attention and be liked through means that are inappropriate in a general education classroom environment. However, the thoughtful care of his teaching team supports him in accumulating positive experience as a capable student in the classroom.

After the whole class phonics lesson, Mrs. Chen gathers a small group of students, including Paul, over to her table to begin their reading group instruction for the day. While this happens, the remainder of the class works independently on their daily reading assignment. As is common in students with profiles similar to Paul's, a small group of peers tends to yield itself to more productive social opportunities than a whole class group. Paul is in a group with four other students, who are paired at his reading level and working on similar comprehension skills, and are also good social peers.

In this small group, the expectations are consistent and clearly laid out. Paul knows what to expect each day when his reading group meets. Mrs. Chen and Paul have worked to create a relationship over the course of the school year. In addition to chatting with Paul about Pokemon, which Mrs. Chen has taken some time to learn about, they have a mutual love of cats, both having a pet at home. They like to share cat stories with one another. This relationship with Mrs. Chen is invaluable. It bonds Paul to his classroom teacher, providing a sense of security and a connection to learning. Though the reading group is not successful every day, Paul wants it to be. His relationship with Mrs. Chen provides incentive for Paul to work for her.

Mrs. Chen's weekly consult with the therapeutic inclusion special education teacher, Mrs. Tabor, and therapist, Mr. Twomey, keeps her abreast of developments with Paul. Through this meeting, Mrs. Chen is able to discuss how Paul is progressing in the general education classroom environment. The team is able to make any necessary changes to the benefit of Paul, Mrs. Chen, or other students in the classroom.

At one weekly consult, Mrs. Chen and Mrs. Tabor determined that when Paul is successfully attending to his reading group, Mrs. Tabor can be available to aid students working independently on their reading assignments, providing assistance and on-the-spot teaching as necessary. This frees up Mrs. Chen to focus on the students that she is working with within her small group.

While in reading group with his peers, Paul is not only afforded the transition time to and from his group to chat with his peers, he is provided with social opportunities embedded into his learning. The students in Paul's reading group, including Paul, have excellent decoding skills. They do not need additional targeted phonics instruction, and so they are a part of a comprehension-based reading group. These students do not have a comprehension deficit, they are all reading on grade level and therefore afforded the ability to be part of a book group.

Mrs. Chen has developed a reading group that yields itself to rich discussions of text that students read independently during their reading block. Students are able to make connections to other literature, their own lives and experiences, and the world around them. This type of learning is especially significant for Paul. Accessing learning throughout his school career has been challenging at times due to his behavior, and he often did not have the opportunity to truly demonstrate his knowledge base in front of his peers. Most days, when Paul is regulated and able to access his book group, Paul feels very successful as a student. He is able to connect with his classmates on an intellectual level and truly showcase his knowledge.

Academic opportunities

Paul's reading group in the general education environment allows him the opportunity to begin to redefine his view of himself, no longer a failure in the classroom, and begin to build his self-worth as a student. Moreover, this reading group, made possible through the collaboration between Mrs. Chen and the Oak teaching team, alongside the security provided by Paul's membership in the Oak Program, is an academic opportunity that is rich and meaningful—one that he would not be able to receive in a substantially separate environment.

With the inclusive opportunities provided for Paul, he is truly a member of two classroom communities: Mrs. Chen's classroom and the Oak classroom. Paul requires both environments to have a safe and productive school day in the least restrictive environment. While the Oak classroom affords many opportunities for its student members, the general education classroom is the environment where the most rigorous academics take place. The Oak cohort does not provide a peer group at Paul's instructional comprehension level to be able to have book talks and provide extensions to the curriculum in the same way that Mrs. Chen's classroom can.

It is extremely important that members of the Oak Program are receiving appropriately challenging academic instruction, and not being given watered-down curriculum or expectations as a result of their disability, behavior, or membership in the Oak Program.

It's also important to mention that simply being with a diverse and rigorous peer group provides a venue for academic conversation and learning that is not easily available in a small group. The student-to-student model accounts for a huge amount of the learning occurring each day. Being exposed to, and successful within, one's peer group is the only way this kind of learning can be accessed.

Though often a result of well-meaning individuals, students with emotional disabilities, or with other profiles who are placed in a therapeutic inclusion program often do not receive an appropriately challenging curriculum. Students with a history of emotional or behavioral challenges in a school environment often have a complex set of needs. Before being identified for a program, these students are rarely provided with wrap-around supports that address their social, emotional, and/or behavioral needs to the extent that they require to make them available for academic learning.

As a result, well-intentioned educators do not often challenge these students academically in the same way that they would with their peers who do not present with these behaviors. There are a variety of reasons why this may occur. Educators may feel that by presenting challenging curriculum and instruction to students they may "set them off," a term frequented by general and special educators without expertise in students with behavioral challenges. Additionally, staff making curricular decisions regarding these students may not be able to tease out how much their behavior is interfering with their learning, yielding an inaccurate profile of the student's potential. In these instances, it is most likely that the student is given instruction *below* their academic potential.

While it is important that students are able to feel successful as learners, providing them with work that is below their current instructional level, while their peers are receiving adequately challenging work, is not beneficial to this end goal. In fact, it often makes students feel misunderstood. They may believe their teachers believe them to be stupid or not able to do what their peers can do. Accurate or not, these thoughts can be quite easily internalized by the student.

By creating a secure home base that allows students to access as much of the general education classroom curriculum as possible, students are able to meet their academic potential. These individualized circumstances provide academic opportunities for our students that simply are not available in a therapeutic school or fully substantially separate program.

Fostering collaborative relationships

It has been previously mentioned that in order for students who are members of a therapeutic inclusion program to be successful in the general education environment, they need the secure home base of the therapeutic milieu. In the general education classroom, an authentic relationship with the classroom teacher will extend the sense of security. In order for the student to feel like a meaningful, productive member of their classroom, this is imperative.

A fundamental component of creating a therapeutic inclusion program is to foster collaborative relationships between general education teachers and the program staff. Once a program has been developed and running in a school for a number of years, these relationships will be formed and it will be a more seamless collaborative process. When developing a program, or when working with teachers who have not previously worked with the program, it is important to welcome them and patiently introduce them to how the program functions. A thorough introduction to the program, focusing on the overarching goals for students, is important.

Currently in public schools, general education teachers are expected to teach a wide array of students in their classrooms, ranging vastly in linguistic diversity, disability, socioeconomic status, cultural and racial diversity. They must also contend with a wide range of home experiences that equip students differently and unequally for accessing the learning environment. Despite these expectations, most teachers do not have the experience of working with students in a specialized social–emotional program, particularly a therapeutic milieu.

When working with general education teachers, one will run across a variety of skill levels and openness for partnering with the program at hand. However, with an authentic relationship with the therapeutic inclusion team, any teacher can be a successful partner in a therapeutic inclusion program.

When describing the program, it is important that teachers are aware of the following tenets:

> The emotional care of the student is equally as important as the academic learning that will occur. These do not compete with one another, they, most often, happen in tandem.
>
> You, the general education teacher, are the child's teacher. It is vital that they feel a relationship with you and authentic membership in your classroom community.
>
> We, the therapeutic inclusion professional staff and the general education teacher are here to work in a partnership. Together we can hold the student emotionally, develop social relationships, and provide rigorous and positive academic programming. In our partnership, we support your teaching in the general education classroom.

General education teachers come to value this partnership. In a collaborative team, the therapeutic inclusion program staff can bring therapeutic and relationship-based experience and expertise to the general education classroom which aids not only the students in the program, but also the teacher and class as a whole.

Meetings

It is essential to develop a regular meeting time with each general education teacher with whom the program collaborates. Typically, 30 minutes one time per week is sufficient. While these meetings do not need to be rigid in their agenda or design, the following items will usually be discussed:

Check-in with the general education teacher to see how things are going from their perspective.

Any changes in schedule or special programming that may be occurring in either environment.

An update from the therapeutic inclusion team revolving around shared students. This is a great time to share appropriate updates from the weekly parent consult, communication books, and anything that seems to be bubbling to the surface with any student.

Academic concerns or data sharing of recent assessments or observations in the classroom.

Social or emotional concerns that the teacher is noticing from their perspective.

These meetings are a useful time to share information, help the team maintain appropriate consistency in their approaches with students, and brainstorm any changes that may need to be made. Weekly meetings allow the teacher to be able to have a more complete picture of the student, often strengthening the teacher–student relationship. These meetings are essential for integration for both the therapeutic inclusion program students and the program teaching team into the general education environment.

Impromptu check-ins between the general education teacher and program staff will occur as well. Generally, the more communication that occurs, the better. It is not necessary to hold information for the weekly consultation meeting that may be valuable to pass on beforehand.

A meeting between Oak Program staff and Mrs. Chen

At 8:00 on a Tuesday morning, 45 minutes before school begins, Mr. Twomey and Mrs. Tabor walk up to the third-grade classroom to meet with Mrs. Chen. It's December, and these three team members have been meeting weekly to discuss their shared students. The meetings have become comfortable and efficient.

"Before I forget …" Mrs. Chen begins. She provides a math assessment that she is going to administer later that week. One of their shared students receives all assessments administered one-to-one in a quiet room as an accommodation on his IEP. Mrs. Tabor and Mrs. Chen check in briefly about the curriculum for the upcoming week.

Subsequently, Mr. Twomey asks Mrs. Chen how things are going in the classroom from her perspective. Mrs. Chen relays that, overall, things are going well, but Paul seems to be having a difficult time during math lately, especially at the end of the block before going to lunch. Mr. Twomey responds that Ms. LaChance, an Oak paraprofessional, has noticed this as well. The conversation continues, in order to integrate multiple perspectives of what Paul's difficult time looks like. Mr. Twomey also notes that this block of time is right before Paul goes to the nurse to receive his medication for the afternoon. The team decides to have Paul take a movement break in the middle of math, with the aid of Ms. LaChance. This will happen in between Mrs. Chen's whole group instruction and when the class begins their independent math work. Mr. Twomey tells Mrs. Chen that he will relay this information to Paul's parents during their consult tomorrow, as Paul has recently had a growth spurt and may need to consider dosage adjustment for his medication.

Mrs. Chen brings up another student that she has concerns about, who is a general education student currently receiving no special education services or intervention. This student is having a very difficult time with written output during Mrs. Chen's writing blocks. Mrs. Tabor is currently providing push-in services for another student, Anthony, at that time and offers to utilize the opportunity to take a small group to Mrs. Chen's table once her mini-lesson is done and the students are working on their writing. She asks Mrs. Chen if there are one or two other students who could benefit from additional support while writing, and they create a small group, including Anthony.

This is a typical, albeit productive, example of a meeting between the Oak staff and a general education teacher. When used thoughtfully, these meetings serve all members of the teaching team, as well as all students in the program and in the classroom.

Integration into the general education environment

When students are integrated into the general education environment, various levels of support will be necessary. This level of support can vary day to day, and also quite significantly from student to student. Some students require support during all of the times that they are integrated into the general education environment, while others do not.

Given the level of demand for an activity, considering both social and academic expectations, there are students who can be successful in the general education environment without the presence of a staff member from the therapeutic inclusion program. This can occur during small portions of the day, such as snack time. It can also occur for larger chunks of the day, such as a reading group, for students whose academic needs, tolerance, and preference for said task do not require individualized support.

A student's need for support from the therapeutic inclusion team must be evaluated on an individualized basis. The ability to provide a student time in the general education setting unsupported by program staff provides logistical easement when determining staffing and scheduling, while providing students the opportunity to feel successful and able. When rebuilding students' view of themselves as learners, their ability to be independently successful, when possible, is a significant piece of the puzzle.

When a member of the therapeutic inclusion staff is supporting students in the general education environment, there are a variety of roles that staff members can take. These roles are not fixed, and will shift depending on the presentation of the program student and the classroom at any given moment. These roles include:

- 1:1 assistance
- Small group assistance
- Small group teaching
- Co-teaching
- Lead teaching (with the general education teacher assisting individually, or working with a small group including the student(s) in the therapeutic inclusion program).

Determining what role the program staff will take in the general education environment is dependent on a variety of factors. The first is student need. If a student is new to general education or struggling with regulation or safety issues in the general education environment, the therapeutic inclusion staff member will need to focus one-to-one on that student in order to guide success in that environment. This is the most restrictive approach to be taken within the context of the general education environment, which is of course still less restrictive than being in a substantially separate environment. This approach may be necessary during a transition or during difficult periods that surface with a student or students.

Given the makeup of students that are in both the therapeutic inclusion program and general education environment together, it may be necessary to have a similar situation, where the staff member is focusing on self-regulation and group participation in the general education environment, but with two or more students. It is also possible, depending on the needs of program students, that the program staff member will be able to provide less intensive small group assistance, allowing them to circulate around the room and check-in with other members of the class, while still providing support to the program students.

Other models which provide less intensive support from a therapeutic inclusion staff member to program students in the general education environment can include small group teaching, co-teaching, or even lead teaching in the classroom. Typically, these situations can occur when the program students are comfortable members of the classroom, and able to be regulated with the presence of a therapeutic inclusion staff member and more limited support. These models are also dependent on both the general education teacher's preference and level of collaboration with the therapeutic inclusion team, and the program staff member's levels of skill and expertise.

Members of a therapeutic inclusion program team will include a therapist, a special education teacher, and paraprofessionals. The special education teacher will have the training and experience to teach whole or small group lessons, and should also be familiar with a co-teaching model. When collaborating successfully, the general education teacher and special educator can determine how to structure lessons and instruction to best fit the needs of all of their students, both those in the program and the remainder of the students in the classroom. When well utilized, the collaboration of a general education and special education teacher in the classroom will provide a truly enriching learning experience to the entire class.

When the program therapist is supporting in the general education classroom, there are multiple roles for that individual as well. In addition to one-to-one or small group support for students in the therapeutic inclusion program, the therapist can provide significant support to the classroom teacher and classroom as a whole. This can take the form of providing whole class targeted psychoeducation lessons, similar to what a typical school counselor may provide. This could utilize a formal curriculum, such as Zones of Regulation® or Social Thinking®, or this could be more dynamic and specifically targeted to the group needs. The therapist is also available to respond to events that may arise throughout the day.

The role that a paraprofessional can take in the general education environment will vary largely based on the experience and motivation of the individual at hand. Paraprofessionals may be certified special education teachers, who are trained and interested in taking on additional responsibilities. In this case, the paraprofessional may take a role similar to the special educator in the program. It is also possible that the paraprofessional will only take the role of supporting students in the therapeutic inclusion program academically and behaviorally, and not provide any novel or lead instruction.

Determining what model to utilize in the classroom will largely be a decision among the teaching team. Levels of expertise, comfort, and the degree of communication and collaboration within the team will all be determining factors. It is important that the therapeutic inclusion team approaches their role in the general education classroom with thoughtful consideration. Classroom teachers put significant time, thought, and care into developing their classroom culture and norms. It is vital that the classroom teacher feels as though the therapeutic inclusion team is coming into the classroom and adding to the experience of both the teacher and the students, not taking over. The program staff aims to help the general education teacher realize that teacher's vision for their classroom.

Generally, it is best to cultivate a collaborative culture with a "we're all in this together" attitude and approach. Being "all in this together" means that the various specialized expertise of members of the team are respected, while roles are flexible enough for staff to respond to the demands of the moment in any combination of academic and social, emotional, and behavioral needs.

Ideally, the general education teacher will be open and comfortable co-teaching with members of the therapeutic inclusion team, as well as taking a support role with program students while the special educator or therapist teaches whole group lessons. This model provides a dynamic teaching team and provides an additional way to integrate program students into the general education classroom while reducing the stigma of being in a program with specialized staff.

Program destigmatization

With thoughtful care and planning, beginning with many of the aforementioned relationships and opportunities presented through the general education classroom, a therapeutic inclusion program can be integrated into the school without disability stigmatization. Other factors to take into consideration include the following.

Program naming

When naming a therapeutic inclusion program, it is important to choose a name that does not arrive with special education or social/emotional/behavioral learning connotations. The program name should be an appealing and otherwise blank marker, which will take on meaning within the school based on the culture of the community that develops. The options for program names will vary between communities. Some examples of program names include Oak, Bridge, and Brook.

Room placement

Ideally, the therapeutic inclusion program should have a room in the main corridor of the school, near grade-level general education classrooms. When building a therapeutic inclusion program, physical space should be carefully considered. Programs often, by default, get placed in an outlier room that is tucked away from the rest of the school. This should be avoided.

A therapeutic inclusion program can benefit from an additional room, which can be used flexibly. This room can be used for many purposes including weekly parent phone calls, small group activities, 1:1 instruction, and conversations which benefit from a quiet uninterrupted space. The room can also be a safer space for a student who is very escalated. It is wise to furnish this room lightly and flexibly, so that it can be quickly converted for various purposes. This room must *not* serve as a space for students outside the program who are highly escalated, due to the stigmatizing message such an arrangement would carry.

Inclusion within therapeutic program classroom

"Reverse inclusion" is a term in use to describe when students from the general education environment are taken to a special education space for instruction provided by a special educator. Reverse inclusion is good practice, but a problematic term that suggests that students with IEPs are backwards, or "reverse." It is better understood simply as inclusion taking place in the special education classroom. In the therapeutic inclusion program classroom, it is the students outside the program that are being included.

This model can be largely beneficial both for students who receive special education services and for those who do not. Pairing students in a therapeutic inclusion program with one or more peers can provide a small group for instruction when otherwise the student would be receiving one-to-one instruction. This arrangement provides an opportunity for peer modeling and allows students to be able to learn together in a way that usually works well both academically and socially.

Inclusion in the therapeutic inclusion program classroom can be of great benefit to general education students. The general education students included would otherwise be one of a large group, typically 20 or more. Being pulled out in a very small group to work on skills allows for responsive and targeted interventions which are more difficult to deliver in the general education classroom.

Open door policy

Often, particularly in an elementary school environment, students are curious about other classrooms where they see some students go, but do not get to go themselves. If indulged thoughtfully, students from the general education classroom will be able to visit, learn, and/or play in the therapeutic inclusion classroom. When this happens, students learn that the separate classroom is a fun place to be, but also not that different from their own classroom. This creates some enthusiasm and positive feeling, while diminishing the mystique of the program classroom. An open door policy for peers and staff is helpful for program destigmatization. The only time the classroom is closed to nonprogram members is during meeting.

Disability awareness

Disability awareness may look and feel different depending on the age and comfort of the students with which you are working. It is also vital to consider student confidentiality. However, students at the elementary level can be told that though we are all similar in many ways, we are also different and have a variety of strengths and weaknesses. The lens of "everyone is working on different things" is a simple and helpful way for students to view difficulties that may arise for students in a therapeutic inclusion program.

Some students in the program may be aware of their disabilities and want to share with their peers. If there is a level of comfort in the student and their families, this should be embraced and used as a springboard to discuss disability awareness and difference acceptance in the classroom. Thoughtfully managed, this can be a very positive part of classroom culture.

Conclusion

There are tremendous inclusion opportunities possible with students who have social, emotional, and behavioral needs, when the students have the security of a therapeutic inclusion program community, and a secure home base in the form of the program classroom. With this in place, students are able to build relationships with their general education teachers and spend significant, rich, and meaningful academic and social time with their peers.

Collaborative, positive relationships with general education teachers are central to a therapeutic inclusion program's success. Authentic and attuned relationships with general education staff should be cultivated, presenting the program as a support to the classroom teacher and general education environment. This is crafted through regular and thoughtful communication. The authentic and responsive relationship therapeutic program staff forms with general education staff is in parallel process with the relationships the general education teacher forms with the program students. The staff of a therapeutic inclusion program supports a meaningful, productive environment for the students in their program, while also elevating the classroom culture and learning for all students in the classroom. By collaborating to cultivate a welcoming environment in both the general education classroom and the therapeutic inclusion classroom, students will be able to feel supported and successful in both environments, contributing to non-stigmatized, full integration of the therapeutic inclusion program into the school culture.

This responsive integration delivers students with significant social, emotional, and behavioral difficulties the inclusion they deserve but rarely receive. Rigorous academics and rich social experiences are available to our therapeutic inclusion program students in the general education environment. Program students can excel in their strengths and showcase their skills. The program student and their peers experience first hand that, for example, the student who often needs help due to feeling emotionally overwhelmed is also very sharp at math. This helps the program student develop a sophisticated self-image and self-esteem and helps their classroom peers witness the amazing diversity of what individuals can contribute to a group.

References

Allen, K. E., & Cowdery, G. E. (2012). *The exceptional child: Inclusion in early childhood education.* Wadsworth Cengage Learning.

Education for All Handicapped Children Act (Public Law 94-142) Individuals with Disabilities Education Act, 20 U.S.C. § 1400 (2004) www.congress.gov/bill/108th-congress/house-bill/1350?q=H.R.+1350+%28108%29

Pearpoint, J., Forest, M., & Snow, J. (1992). *The Inclusion Papers: Strategies to make inclusion work: A collection of articles from the centre.* Inclusion Press.

Salend, S. J. (2007). *Creating inclusive classrooms: Effective and reflective practices* (6th ed.). Pearson.

5 Learning as a Healing Experience

For our therapeutic inclusion program students, responsive, relationship-based care is a continuous part of their school day. The therapeutic responsiveness of the program does not switch on and off depending on the activity or time of the school day.

Due to previous experiences of school failure, incoming therapeutic program students usually arrive with poor self-images of themselves as learners. They often have negative associations with school and school staff. Within the responsive relationships formed in the therapeutic inclusion program, academic work becomes another opportunity for healing. Every time a student is therapeutically supported in feeling successful with academic work, their self-image, and relationship to learning can develop positively. Students will also experience academic challenges within therapeutic relationships, make errors, and/or have difficulty understanding. In this case the task within the responsive staff relationship is to empathize with the difficult feelings, and over time to support the student in valuing and loving themselves in the face of both challenge and success.

In the day-to-day experience, the progress is cumulative and incremental. Furthermore, each student has a unique and often complex self-image, and relationship to school. The therapeutic approach to academic work is always a topic of consideration and adjustment, and the subject of ongoing conversation in therapeutic supervision. This chapter describes the approach and the philosophy at work within the therapeutic inclusion program. Interspersed are six vignettes to help ground the descriptions and theory in the school environment.

Pathways to the therapeutic inclusion program

Students arrive to a therapeutic inclusion program with their own narrative, and family narrative, of the path that brought them there. While students come from a variety of settings, most have internalized significant failure as students and learners. A core therapeutic process within the program is the students' ongoing accumulation of a new sense of themselves as learners and classmates. Therapeutic program staff members and collaborators use their relationships and the therapeutic milieu to facilitate healing and progress.

DOI: 10.4324/9781003270478-6

In our experience in public education, it is generally held that clear-cut entrance criteria for program entry is best practice. At the same time, the complexity and diversity of profiles for students who may be well-placed in the therapeutic inclusion program creates a special challenge. A criteria that is too rigid is likely to lead to errors in program entry determination. Conversely, a vague entrance criteria can be unhelpful to parents and colleagues seeking to understand whether the program might be appropriate for a student. (A sample entrance criteria is offered in Appendix A.)

While meeting the entry criteria for the program is a basis for placement, students will arrive to the therapeutic inclusion program in a variety of ways. This includes, but is not limited to, the student being identified with an emotional disability prior to their elementary school start and being placed into a program from preschool, the student moving school districts with an individualized education program that requires a therapeutic inclusion program or similar, or from the student experiencing failure in their current placement in public school.

Transitioning into the program

Just as every individual is unique, so is every therapeutic relationship. The intention of the therapeutic inclusion program is to truly see each student, and to care and educate each individual with a specialized response. This starts from the family's first contact with the program. With consultation with colleagues and therapeutic supervision, there is ample room for creativity. That being said, there are some elements of student entry to the program that are generally recommended.

- The program co-leaders should observe the student in their previous education environment if possible.
- The program co-leaders should read all previous evaluations and documentation and share salient documentation with the rest of the program staff.
- The program co-leaders should meet with parents to collect information, introduce the program, and start to form working relationships. The program co-leader who will lead parent communication for the new family can take on most of the parent work, after initial introduction to the co-leaders.
- When a child joins the program midyear they should be gradually introduced to the program. The time between initially informing the student about joining the program, to full schedule integration, takes about two weeks on average.
- A social story should be created and shared with the current therapeutic inclusion program members to introduce the new student, as well as the timeline of their gradual entry to the program.
- An additional social story should be created and shared with the new student which introduces the program and the group, as well as the planned timeline for gradual entry into the program.

- The joining student should begin with a visit to the therapeutic inclusion program classroom when it is empty, followed by a visit when other students are present. They can then be introduced to the first chronological part of their school day, morning circle. From there, the student should build their day, adding time in the therapeutic inclusion room.

Whether the student joins the therapeutic inclusion program from within the school, or whether this is an alternate school placement has an effect on the remainder of their introduction. Students who are joining the program from within the school will already be established members of a general education classroom. Additional time within the therapeutic inclusion room, including meeting, will be added to their day. Students who are joining the therapeutic inclusion program from an alternate school will need to establish membership both in the therapeutic inclusion classroom and a grade level corresponding general education classroom. This may be done chronologically through the school day, or the student may require additional time in the therapeutic inclusion classroom as they begin to navigate their new placement, adding incremental time in their general education classroom until they reach their intended schedule.

- In order to encourage a sense of positive gain for students while joining the program, a labeled desk when they first arrive promotes a sense of ownership and belonging. The desk can contain some items such as a pencil box, special pencils, erasers, and a sketch pad.
- In the event that a student joins the program midyear, the program counselor should take one to one time to introduce the basics of meeting (group psychotherapy), with the same content as the group instruction about meeting that occurs at the beginning of the school year.

Brian

Brian came to kindergarten at his neighborhood school, which housed a therapeutic inclusion program. For two years prior, he attended the town's integrated preschool. He has been on an IEP since he was three years old and is currently diagnosed through the school with a developmental delay. His disability category of developmental delay encompasses a "limited, impaired, or delayed learning capacity due to difficulties in social, emotional, or adaptive functioning" (Massachusetts Department of Elementary and Secondary Education, *Developmental Delay* 2006).

While he was in preschool, Brian's developmental delay presented as an inability to make connections with peers. He was rigid and did not want to follow other's plans in play, when he attempted to play with other students at all. When interacting with other children, Brian would often growl at them and showcased regular physical aggression. Brian did not respond well to typical redirection from his preschool teachers and would growl and aggress at them when they would intervene. Brian had both consultation and direct service from the district's BCBA during his time in preschool, which minimized the frequency of his outbursts, yet he did not make significant social or emotional progress during this time. As Brian's IEP team looked ahead to kindergarten, they considered a placement in the therapeutic inclusion program. The school principal and therapeutic inclusion co-leaders were consulted. After reading Brian's background documentation, the co-leaders visited the preschool for observations and consulted with his preschool team. After consideration, Brian's IEP team determined that he would be placed in the therapeutic inclusion program for his kindergarten year.

At the end of his preschool year, the therapeutic inclusion team began to prepare both the current group and Brian for his start in the program in the fall. Social stories were written for the group that included pictures of Brian, his interests, and the plan for Brian to join the therapeutic milieu when the new school year began in September. The therapeutic inclusion team also visited Brian at his preschool so that he could become familiar with his soon-to-be teachers. They brought a social story that they had made that included pictures of the therapeutic inclusion classroom and Brian's future classmates and teachers for Brian to take home and read over the summer. The counselor in the therapeutic inclusion program started to form a relationship with Brian's parents in order to help ease the transition from preschool into elementary school.

Developing authentic and therapeutic relationships

Though innate for many people, the best way to develop meaningful and authentic relationships with children is through curiosity surrounding their thoughts, beliefs, and interests. In doing so, often shared interests will emerge, which are a wonderful springboard for a relationship. When children have interests that are different from the teacher's, this is also a great opportunity for connection. The teacher can bring fresh curiosity to the topic, and the child will feel valued as they have something special about which to teach and share.

Establishing credibility is necessary while building authentic relationships with students. In a traditional teaching role, this may fall largely to being a content expert and delivering material clearly and thoughtfully. However, as an educator in a therapeutic inclusion program, proving oneself to be a credible educator includes content and pedagogy knowledge, but also the ability to take care of students in a way that is unique to individuals requiring this program. Students in our care both require and deserve to know that they will be taken care of socially, emotionally, and physically each day. Staff in the therapeutic inclusion program preview new and/or unexpected changes for students every day, which communicates respect, and contributes to a sense of predictability. Students must experience the thoughtfulness and care of the program staff in order to establish the program as their secure base. Being predictable and following through creates that sense of reliability, thoughtfulness, and caring. Teacher credibility for educators in this program requires some humility. Acknowledging mistakes and errors and discussing them on a human level is another invaluable way to build and maintain relationships with students.

Charles

Charles is a fourth-grade student who had been in a social–emotional learning program in his previous school in another state. His family, due to a job transfer, moved to a town that housed a therapeutic inclusion program within the public school system. Based on address, Charles would have typically attended a different elementary school in the town. Due to the requirements of his IEP, the school district believed he should attend the therapeutic inclusion program and the school that houses it.

Charles' family had a move-in meeting with the co-leaders of the therapeutic inclusion program, as well as the building principal and his future fourth-grade general education teacher. The team discussed Charles' current IEP, his current presentation and familial concerns, and the therapeutic inclusion program. At this meeting, it was determined that this was the least restrictive placement for Charles, and his transition into the program began. This transition occurred unexpectedly and in the middle of the school year, which is nonideal but certainly feasible, and at times necessary in a public school setting. A transition plan was made with the therapeutic inclusion team and Charles' family.

Charles' family had the right for Charles to begin in the therapeutic inclusion program immediately with full days, however, it was determined that a gradual introduction to his new program and school would be best, especially given his diagnosis and presentation of anxiety. Charles had previously experienced significant school refusal, and the team, led by his parents, developed an approach that seemed likely to yield the most successful start to his new school experience. The group was read a social story that a new student, Charles, would be joining their group. They were told that he would be starting a little bit at a time, to get used to school, and hopefully soon he would be at school all day.

Charles' transition to the therapeutic inclusion program began with a video chat with the therapist and teacher in the program. They then moved to a home visit, where the program staff brought toys of interest to Charles and had a casual visit in his own, comfortable environment.

Charles then began coming to school, only in the therapeutic inclusion classroom, not yet spending time in his grade-level general education class. Once Charles was able to comfortably spend an entire school day in the therapeutic inclusion classroom, he was slowly and thoughtfully introduced to his general education classroom with the support of now-familiar program staff.

It starts with an initial "secure base" relationship

As students come to the program with failure and shame, listening to students becomes the basis of every relationship. Students may arrive with an inability to complete any academic tasks or to stay safe throughout even a single school day. These are significant problems within the realm of a public school, and the first step to improving the school experience for these students is to listen to their experience so students will feel heard, and eventually, understood and cared for. Until a student creates a trusting relationship, repair of these challenges that manifest as behaviors such as work refusal and aggression is unlikely.

Within the therapeutic relationship, emotional repair is possible. This will often happen within a primary relationship with a member of the therapeutic inclusion program staff with whom the student can initially connect. It is often the program therapist, but it does not have to be. This relationship may coincide with the staff member with whom the student spends the majority of their time, but that is also not obligatory. Relationships develop authentically and naturally over time, allowing students to gravitate toward and build relationships with staff whom they trust.

In *Better Late Than Never*, Lorraine Price describes the therapeutic relationship as one where the individual in receipt of care can begin to release former maladaptive behaviors.

> When a new and significant dyadic relationship is formed with the therapist these resistances come into the relationship and can be re-experienced, understood, and finally given up. It then becomes possible to experience a new, formative relationship with the therapist.
>
> (2016, p. 100)

This is the hope for students in a school setting. Beginning with one reparative relationship, students can begin to reimagine themselves as students and reform their experience to one that is more positive and does not carry the weight of failure and shame.

Once a therapeutic relationship has been established with a staff member, creating a secure home base, the student is able to realize and understand that trusted adults can exist within a school setting. School does not have to be a place of failure, let down, and failed relationships. The security of the student's primary relationship eventually allows them to try forming relationships with other adults within the school setting. The student learns that they can, indeed, trust themselves to be open and emotionally vulnerable at school with trusted adults, as program staff has shown that they can be taken care of.

Kelsey

Kelsey attends her local, neighborhood elementary school. She has gone to this school since kindergarten. During her kindergarten year, through a referral through the school, Kelsey was given a full battery of special education testing including cognitive, academic achievement, occupational therapy, and speech and language. As a result of this initial special education evaluation, Kelsey was diagnosed with a developmental delay and began to receive special education services in reading, math, occupational therapy, and speech and language. Kelsey had behavioral episodes where she would refuse work. When prompted to complete her work, she would begin to throw or kick things in her environment, and at times become physically aggressive toward adults. These issues increased as her kindergarten year progressed.

When Kelsey began in Ms. Lampbert's first-grade class, her maladaptive behavior increased significantly. Though it is difficult to be confident about what accounted for an increase in aggressive behavior, the workload expectations, which were difficult for Kelsey, increased significantly with first grade. At this point, Kelsey was having frequent (multiple times per week) aggressive and unsafe outbursts directed at adults, attempting to inflict bodily harm on multiple occasions.

The school counselor began to work with Kelsey, providing individual sessions once a week for 30 minutes. At the same time, the counselor from the therapeutic inclusion program, Mr. Twomey, began observing Kelsey in order to provide recommendations to her current teaching team. Mr. Twomey made recommendations, noting through these observations that Kelsey was both regularly significantly unsafe at school and also experiencing extreme distress and failure as a student. Kelsey's IEP team convened and made a recommendation for Kelsey to join the therapeutic inclusion program.

As it was fall and Kelsey was already a student in the school belonging to a general education classroom, her full transition into the program happened within two weeks. To begin, the program staff used social stories to introduce the therapeutic inclusion program group to Kelsey, as well as Kelsey to the program and her new program peers. Kelsey then began to visit the classroom, beginning with morning circle. She came for a 15-minute visit, and then her time increased incrementally until she was receiving all of her special education services in the therapeutic milieu. Her former academic services, reading and math, were gradually and thoughtfully shifted from the learning center special education teacher to the therapeutic inclusion special education teacher, Mrs. Tabor, taught in the Oak classroom. Her speech and language and occupational services remained, but these service providers now had regular consultation with the Oak team. Kelsey also continued to spend a significant amount of time in Ms. Lampbert's general education classroom.

As Kelsey began her first-grade year dysregulated and, at times, unsafe in this classroom, it was vital for Kelsey and the Oak team to work to repair the teacher relationships that had been established under difficult circumstances. This was done in a multitude of ways. By providing Kelsey with the therapeutic support that she needed, she was able to be increasingly regulated and safe at school. With therapeutic support in the milieu and in the general education classroom, her presentation while in the general education classroom changed significantly for the better. Additionally, when Kelsey was dysregulated or had occasional unsafe episodes, these occurred with the program staff in the therapeutic milieu as she now had a safe place to retreat. While Kelsey had not yet developed the ability to experience her intense emotions safely, she immediately understood that the therapeutic staff and milieu comprised a safer place to experience these upsetting feelings.

Regular consultation meetings with Kelsey's general education teacher and the Oak team, as well as consistent support for Kelsey throughout the school day, allowed Ms. Lampbert the time and space to be able to better understand her disability and her needs. Ms. Lampbert and Kelsey now had the stability, support, and understanding necessary to repair the relationship that had gotten off to a rocky start. As Kelsey's classmates saw her behavior transform, they were quick to form new relationships as resilient, young children often are.

Reparative relationships in the context of therapeutic education

Though the arrival to a therapeutic inclusion program looks different in each case, once students are members of the therapeutic milieu, there are common themes. These include revisioning oneself as a learner and developing ways to feel successful in the school setting. The work begins by developing a reparative relationship within the milieu.

In order to use the reparative relationship for therapeutic benefit, we first establish an understanding of what a therapeutic relationship can look like in the context of a public school. The concept of the reparative relationship is well known in the realm of psychotherapy, however, it is not well versed in literature, or commonly defined. The concept builds upon the object relations work of Melanie Klein, D.W. Winnicott, and others and is often associated with repairing an injury from the child–parent relationship (Clarkson, 1995).

Object relations theory holds that the primary relationships children develop become an internal image that is in turn applied to future relationships (Segal,

1974). While there are commonalities, each internal image is an imprint of a unique relationship. From their parent(s), children usually internalize images containing a sense of caretaker, authority, and love. If they have a sibling not far from their own age, they begin to develop an image of what a peer is that is also carried forward with them.

As they develop, children build from their primary familial relationships to develop increasingly distinct image of what teachers and school represent. While the caretakers at school change over time, the institution of school is usually the most significant caretaker outside of home. This often starts well before kindergarten, as the child adapts to the rhythm of separating from the parents on weekdays for group childcare and preschool, which many families refer to as "school" when speaking to the child.

In the therapeutic inclusion program, the object relationship that most often requires reparative attention is the child's relationship to teachers and school. This is most often because the school environment was not previously appropriately resourced, structured, and trained to match to the student's needs, and rarely because of a notable deficiency in previous teachers. In the therapeutic inclusion program, the reparative relationship is also used to support the child in repairing their sense of themselves as learners and peers.

For our purposes in the school environment, a reparative relationship is one that works to heal former relationships which have developed in ways that have been problematic for the student. By creating a dependable and trusting relationship starting within the therapeutic milieu, students can feel safe and cared for. This relationship can be a model and springboard for healthy relationships with school staff, peers, and even the institution of school itself, moving forward.

Amir

Amir is a first-grade student in his local elementary school. In preschool he was diagnosed with a developmental delay. He had significant difficulty in his preschool years regulating his emotions at school, with frequent behavioral outbursts, and significant tantrums, wailing and crying for upwards of 30 minutes before calming. He received specialized instruction in preschool, which led to a decrease in his maladaptive behavior.

When it was time for Amir to transition into kindergarten, he did so with a thorough transition plan and behavioral support, but the team did not deem his placement in the therapeutic inclusion program to be the LRE for him at that time. With support in place, and a predictable, experienced kindergarten teacher, Amir had a largely successful kindergarten year.

Amir attended the extended school year program during the summer between his kindergarten and first-grade years in order to help prevent the regression of skills that he had gained. During the extended year program, Amir began to exhibit significant regression. He was having frequent tantrums and extended crying episodes. He had significant work refusal and regressed toward lengthy and remarkably intense tantrums. Amir also exhibited new eloping behavior, leaving the room without permission when he was upset. This change in behavior was documented over the summer program but did not lead to any changes to Amir's transition plan for entering his first-grade year.

In September, Amir began first grade. He presented very similarly to the extended school year program, yielding a difficult transition. Amir's first-grade teacher, Ms. Lieberman, had a very difficult time with his outbursts, becoming overwhelmed and approaching panic when they occurred. As a result, she would often take the remainder of the students out of the classroom when his tantrum behavior began, calling the school's crisis team to intervene.

Ms. Lieberman brought Amir's case to a child study meeting, where his behavior was discussed and interventions were suggested by the school psychologist and school counselor. These suggestions included a behavior plan that Ms. Lieberman could implement, as well as the school counselor teaching once weekly Zones of Regulation™ curriculum to the entire first-grade class. Ms. Lieberman could observe the lessons and integrate them throughout Amir's school day.

These strategies were tried for four weeks, though Ms. Lieberman continued to feel generally overwhelmed by his behavior and was unable to successfully implement his behavior plan. During this time, the school put an additional staff member, a paraprofessional, in Amir's classroom to aid in the implementation of his behavior plan. Amir's behavior did not improve over the course of these four weeks, his work refusal, tantrums, and eloping increased significantly.

After four weeks, the child study team met again. At this point the counselor, Mr. Twomey, and special educator, Mrs. Tabor, from the therapeutic inclusion program were asked to be a part of the meeting. During this meeting, it was determined that additional interventions needed to be put in place. The school counselor determined that she would see Amir once per week in a pull-out model for counseling. The therapeutic inclusion team determined that they would conduct three observations and then offer suggestions to Amir's teachers. Throughout this time, Amir's maladaptive behavior became more frequent and he began eloping multiple times per day and hitting and throwing objects at the paraprofessional who had been tasked with aiding in the classroom. Though the therapeutic inclusion team was able to offer suggestions for Amir's behavior, it was difficult for all of them to be implemented without the support of the therapeutic milieu, and it was an unrealistic burden for the paraprofessional who had been placed in the classroom to carry out this job alone without consistent support from the therapeutic inclusion teaching team. An IEP meeting was called and Amir's placement was changed. His transition to the therapeutic inclusion program began shortly after. Two weeks later, he was fully transitioned into the program.

Recovery from shame and internalized failure

Students who enter a therapeutic inclusion program nearly always arrive harboring feelings of shame, as they have all experienced significant school failure. Though many will not explicitly state this, and may use coping mechanisms for self-protection, they all have experienced school as a place where thriving seems beyond reach. Through the creation of a therapeutic relationship, shame can be diminished as the student is seen and understood within a highly responsive care environment. Within this environment, the child can accumulate experience feeling successful at school. Over the long term, the child reforms their image of themselves as a learner, a peer, and in relationship to school.

Though most staff members in a therapeutic inclusion program are not trained therapists, therapeutic supervision will provide program staff with a clear understanding of the role they play within the milieu. The culture of a therapeutic inclusion program should be built around listening with the intention to understand. When a culture of listening exists, and students are able to feel understood, they receive the message that being a member of the therapeutic inclusion program is not a repeat of a previous experience, but is in fact a new experience. This is when learning begins as a healing process. It is possible for every staff member to be able to do this with the support and guidance of therapeutic supervision.

This is accomplished, in part, by meeting each student where they are. This is a concept frequently touted in the world of early childhood and elementary education. However, it can be hard to execute in a large group such as a general education classroom. The intimacy of a therapeutic milieu provides that opportunity. In this environment, it is not just best practice, it is essential.

Kelsey: Forming a new relationship

Kelsey's arrival to the therapeutic inclusion program, as previously mentioned in this chapter, brought a student who was often angry, at times aggressive, and overall unheard and misunderstood. This is not who Kelsey is at her core. At her core she is a thoughtful, empathetic, intuitive, and funny child. However, her previous school experience had not allowed her to blossom. She had not been given the support that she needed in order to be successful.

Kelsey had, at the age of six, determined that she was not only bad and a failure, but that she was stupid. She came to the program with intense feelings of shame. Kelsey's ability to begin to transform her vision of herself took a lot of time, investment, listening, and sitting with distress on behalf of the program staff. The first relationship that Kelsey made was with the program therapist, Mr. Twomey.

Kelsey and Mr. Twomey had shared a few interactions in Ms. Lampbert's class, as Mr. Twomey was observing and consulting. Now,

Kelsey and Mr. Twomey were working together in earnest. Mr. Twomey and Kelsey worked on establishing a sense of belonging in the therapeutic inclusion program classroom. Kelsey was presented with her school desk, with her name on it. Her desk contained a pencil box with colorful pencils and erasers, a new set of markers, and a blank sketchbook. Later, Kelsey cut out a silhouette of a balloon, decorated it, and wrote her name and birthday on it. This was placed on the birthday wall along with balloons from all the Oak Program members. With each activity, the sense of belonging became increasingly personalized. Kelsey was interested in unicorns, and Mr. Twomey made sure the classroom contained popular books on the topic, as well as toys that fit Kelsey's interests. With these activities, as well as some time talking and playing together, Kelsey and Mr. Twomey formed the beginnings of a therapeutic relationship.

The relationship that was established between Mr. Twomey and Kelsey allowed her to consider that she could, in fact, trust adults in the school environment. This relationship was the beginning of healing for Kelsey. However, she did have a comorbidity of a significant learning disability, leading to her feelings of inadequacy as a student. Through the reparative relationship that was formed with the therapist, Kelsey was able to then create a relationship with the special education teacher, Mrs. Tabor. For the first time, Kelsey felt safe enough to be open and vulnerable about her learning difficulties, most significantly regarding her difficulty learning to read.

Through the relationship that was forged between Kelsey and her special education teacher, Kelsey was able to begin to build reading skills. Mrs. Tabor understood that Kelsey needed to be provided with work that was accessible but did not make her feel younger than she was. She needed to be challenged, but not pushed to the point of frustration. Otherwise, it would be hard for her not to, in her words, "fly into a rage." A delicate balance was struck between taking care of Kelsey's fragile emotional self, who saw reading as something that she was inherently "stupid" at, and adequately challenging her to make effective progress in this academic realm. Most of the time, this went very well and Kelsey made great strides in becoming a reader as well as viewing herself as someone who could have the grit and vulnerability to learn in a school environment.

The therapeutic element is always present

At school, academic learning sessions begin and end, while the therapeutic approach of the program is always in effect. The therapeutic inclusion program staff, with the support of supervision, brings relationship-based therapeutic responsiveness into the milieu, the general education classroom, and throughout the school. This is done with the same sense of intentionality a psychodynamic therapist brings into a dyadic relationship with a client. The therapist's intention is to form a relationship where new conversations are possible, new understanding is possible, where the relationship is safe enough to try different ways of thinking and being.

Within the parallel of the therapeutic inclusion program, academic work is a perhaps surprising asset to this process. Students formulate their self-image as learners in significant part based on how they encounter academic work. Our students with social, emotional, and behavioral difficulties often have less tolerance for error, especially if their self-esteem is already low. Some work avoidance behaviors are driven by the desire to avoid any challenge that might exacerbate an already stinging sense of inadequacy. The task of the program staff is to approach the teaching and academic support in a therapeutic fashion, with factors like these chiefly in mind.

When the student approaches academic work from within a responsive, therapeutic relationship with program staff, a pathway to change in the student's relationship to academic work is opened. The program staff carries this intention into the academic session, alongside the mission to teach and support the academic curriculum. From within this relationship, celebrating academic success, and confronting academic challenge, become meaningful in new ways. With the support of the therapeutic program staff the student can engage in, and experience, repair of their image of themselves as learners (Linda Butler, personal communication, 2008).

Creating reparative relationships in public school settings requires vulnerability from staff as well as the student. Staff can initially feel pressure to "get it right" all of the time. However, typical failures and slip-ups on the part of the program staff are part of the work and are far from catastrophic. In fact, Price (2016) states that "the therapist's occasional and unintentional failure for the client can actually help the client to recognize the normal failures which are a part of life, and to become robust and resilient" (p. 121). This will also be seen within the therapeutic milieu.

Amir: A staff mistake—not a laughing matter

Amir, previously described in this chapter highlighting his arrival to the program, had been a member of the therapeutic inclusion program for about a year and a half. He made a successful transition into the program and was doing significantly better with school. This was noted by his previous year and current general education teachers, his parents, and Amir himself. Amir would self describe as "I used to be bad, but I'm not anymore." Program staff would respond that Amir was never bad, while also acknowledging the previous difficulties he experienced. Over the course of his time in the therapeutic inclusion program, Amir had developed a therapeutic relationship with the program special educator and had been very successful in engaging with work, growing himself as a student and a child.

Amir had social and emotional delays that impacted his communication and interactions. He was also charismatic, likable, and good natured, which led friendly adults and children to humor his social eccentricities. He enjoyed being silly, telling nonsensical stories, and using standard joke formats to tell jokes which were not coherent or understandable. (Readers may have experienced this phenomenon with toddlers playing with the format of a knock-knock joke, for example.) Peers did often respond to his jokes with laughter, but often he was being humored, and sometimes he was unknowingly the subject of the laughter. Under these circumstances, and given his social delays, it was difficult for Amir to recognize that his jokes were not landing as intended.

With Amir's outward behavior improving significantly, and his view of himself as a learner and a student much improved, the program staff felt as though Amir's humor and connection to peers was an area that could be broached. One piece of direct instruction with this work was a lesson on jokes during a pscyhoeducational group. Mrs. Tabor provided a thorough lesson outlining why people tell jokes, knowing your audience, and the elements of a joke. She provided illustrative examples. The students were then given the opportunity to tell their own jokes. Four members of the group made up jokes, some funnier than others, but all involving a pun, unexpected connection, or some element of humor. Amir then raised his hand to tell a joke and said "the bears followed the purple line to get the bacon."

Mrs. Tabor took in Amir's joke and said kindly and clearly "Amir, your joke was not funny, because it didn't make sense." At this point, Amir's face fell very dramatically and he began to cry. The other program staff in the classroom began to silently laugh at the combination of the explicit lesson, terrible joke, and mostly at Mrs. Tabor's well-intentioned error. Though Mrs. Tabor tried extremely hard to keep her composure, she was not able to and also began laughing. Amir, continuing to cry, was very upset at his teacher. Mrs. Tabor apologized in the moment, but this matter was revisited on many occasions.

Amir arrived at school the next day, pointed at Mrs. Tabor, and stated "I'm not talking to her." She assured Amir that it was okay if he didn't want to talk and again apologized for laughing during the group the day before. Mrs. Tabor explained why the moment felt silly to some of the people in the group, and how she laughed too. However, she was very sorry for laughing and wished that she had not. This topic continued to come up over the course of the following weeks.

Mrs. Tabor had significant guilt for not being able to control her impulses and hold back her laughter in this moment. She brought it up during supervision, which was helpful in working through the moment and realizing that, while not her best moment, it was not catastrophic and could be a useful experience for both Amir and his teacher.

Amir was in a deep and trusting relationship with Mrs. Tabor at the time of this disruption. Though very upset initially, he was able to talk and work through the feelings. It was a feeling of upset that had occurred for Amir before, and it was certain to occur at other moments throughout his life and his school career. Having the practice to work through this, and come out with renewed trust for his teacher, was a learning experience for Amir that he could carry forward. The group also benefited from the conversations of repair and care that occurred in the therapeutic milieu around this emotionally rich and complex moment they had co-experienced.

For the therapeutic program staff, the chance to apologize is a special therapeutic opportunity. It demonstrates to the students that the adults can not only "talk the talk," but can also "walk the walk." Apologizing is an act of humility and vulnerability that staff can and should safely engage in and helps to form trusting relationships. When students see that their teachers can be vulnerable and acknowledge mistakes, they feel more able to do the same.

Conclusion

Learning is a therapeutic healing experience for students in a therapeutic inclusion program. This is a core conceptual building block for a program where students have previously internalized significant failure. Though students arrive at a therapeutic inclusion program from different places, all of our students have had severe difficulty tolerating group learning, and a series of upsetting previous learning settings are almost always shared.

Through creating reparative relationships with the program staff, healing for students can begin. All therapeutic program staff members and collaborators, with the support of therapeutic supervision, can use their relationships and the therapeutic milieu to facilitate student healing and progress. By developing reparative relationships and creating a culture around listening to and understanding students, it is possible for the student to receive the message that being a member of the therapeutic inclusion program is not another failed school experience, but a new kind of experience where they are provided with the relationships and healing to be successful.

References

Clarkson, P. (1995). *The therapeutic relationship.* Whurr.

Massachusetts Department of Elementary and Secondary Education. (2006, July 13). *Developmental Delay.* Developmental Delay – Special Education. Retrieved July 30, 2022, from www.doe.mass.edu/sped/links/ddelay.html

Price, L. (2016). *Better late than never: The reparative therapeutic relationship in regression to dependence.* Routledge.

Segal, H. (1964). *Introduction to the work of Melanie Klein.* Basic Books.

6 Curriculum

Navigating Offerings, Opportunities, and Priorities

In order for learning to be a continuation of the therapeutic experience for our students, it should be carefully designed and calibrated to meet each student academically and emotionally. Therapeutic educators have determinations to make between setting, grouping, instructional programs, methodology, and structure of lessons. The starting point in each subject begins with the student's current level of performance paired with the curriculum and educational settings offered by the school.

When the general education setting and/or curriculum is not a fit for the students, this becomes the point of departure where a wide range of choices are available to the therapeutic special educator. We will examine the background, process, and thinking that goes into instructional determinations for students in the therapeutic inclusion program.

This chapter discusses the therapeutic inclusion program's approach to determining curriculum and academic setting while considering the social, emotional, and behavioral needs of our students alongside their learning needs. Flexibility is of special importance in order to faithfully provide the least restrictive learning environment to students with fluctuating and evolving social, emotional, and behavioral presentations. A two-part vignette demonstrates the therapeutic inclusion program's approach in practice.

Academic determinations

Since the early 1990s, public school systems in the United States have been providing mandates for the content that students are responsible for learning throughout their years in the educational system. By the early 2000s, every state had developed its own content learning standards. Having learning standards developed at a statewide level provided challenges as there was a lack of consistency throughout school systems. Additionally, proficiency expectations varied widely nationwide. In an attempt to provide a more consistent public education throughout the country, the Common Core State Standards (CCSS) were adopted in 2009.

Common Core standards outline the content that students are required to demonstrate proficiency in each school year. These standards are cumulative and, upon high school graduation, students should have demonstrated

DOI: 10.4324/9781003270478-7

proficiency in skills which allow them the knowledge and skills to be prepared for adult life, which in many cases includes plans for college. In 2012, states began reviewing and utilizing the Common Core standards. The adoption of CCSS occurred on a voluntary basis. In many, but not all states, the standards were either adopted by school boards or state-level governments. As of the completion of this book, 41 states have implemented the CCSS and are implementing them at their discretion in regard to timing (National Governors Association Center for Best Practices, Council of Chief State School Officers 2010).

Though curriculum content may be mandated, pedagogy, or the way that the content is delivered, is not. There are various ways for teachers to determine how to best teach the students before them in their classrooms. In the therapeutic program the ideal way to do so is by developing a thorough understanding of, and relationship with each student (as covered in detail in Chapter Five). There are various ways that this can be accomplished, many of them inherent to the human experience. Setting aside time to develop an authentic relationship with students is one of the best.

By developing authentic relationships with genuine care teachers will develop trust with students, which is necessary for reluctant students in completing academic work. This relationship, in conjunction with the information provided in a student's formal testing and IEP, will provide insight as to how to best service each student.

Special education determination and placement process

Students who are placed in a therapeutic inclusion program will be determined to have a disability. This may be an emotional disability, a neurological disability which impacts their ability to regulate emotions and behavior, or a combination. For example, a student diagnosed with ADHD may present with an extreme level of reactivity and sensitivity that has a neurological basis, presenting with deficits in impulse control, attention, and social ability necessary to be successful without the support that is offered through the therapeutic milieu. If a student has a disability and is unable to make effective progress in school without additional supports, an IEP will be developed for the student.

An IEP will be developed based on a variety of components. This will include parental concerns and input, classwork samples, teacher observations, as well as informal and formal assessments. The formal assessments which will be conducted are determined by the IEP team and can include academic achievement, psychological, speech and language, behavior, and occupational therapy assessments, among other possibilities. The result of these components provides a current level of education performance and a basis for a student's IEP. Based on these factors, the IEP team will determine whether a student requires accommodations and/or modifications to the curriculum.

Accommodations throughout a student's day allow them to receive grade-level content instruction while being provided with tools and strategies to access the curriculum. Some examples of accommodations that could be helpful to students with disabilities are providing visuals to accompany auditory learning, providing directions in one to two steps at a time, and pre-teaching vocabulary that may be critical and novel to the lesson. Accommodating the curriculum for students does not change the learning outcome.

For students with more intensive learning needs, modifications are often needed. Providing a modification means that a *change* will be made to the content or proficiency outcomes in order to meet a student's needs. If a student's disability or current level of education performance determines that they are unable to access grade-level curriculum standards, even with adaptations and specialized instruction, they will be provided with a modified education program.

As a teacher, a student's IEP provides a template for beginning to approach a student's academic needs. In addition to evaluating the need for accommodations and possible modifications, and in which particular subject areas, the IEP will dictate how much support students receive from specialist teachers. Based on a student's level of need, and determined by their IEP, a student may receive services from, but not limited to, a special education teacher, occupational therapist, physical therapist, speech and language pathologist, counselor, psychologist, and/or behavior interventionist. These services will be tied to particular goals and may take place either within a student's general educational environment or individually or within small groups outside of the general education classroom.

Determining setting

Determining *where* a student's services will take place is as vital as deciding *what* and *how* a student will learn. In the therapeutic inclusion program model, along with any other special education services, there are two basic environments where a student can be present: *in* the general education environment and *out of* the general education environment. While in the general education environment, students are with their grade-level peers and general education teacher. In this environment, students can be independent or they can be provided support from special educators or related service staff, such as an occupational therapist or speech-language pathologist. When students are out of the general education environment, their services are delivered in another location. In this environment, students are only with a special educator or related service provider either one-to-one or in a small group, most often consisting of other students with special education services.

There are benefits to both models of instruction. Providing special education services within a student's general education classroom allows the opportunity for the student to be a part of their larger community. They receive the same curricular content as their peers while also being provided with additional tools and resources from specialist teachers. Students may receive a short mini-lesson, where a teacher provides grade-level content to the whole class, and then work individually or within a small group with a specialist teacher to apply the skills and knowledge that they have just learned alongside their class. Additionally, the specialist teacher has the opportunity to work on the student's goals for their content area in a generalized setting. For example, an occupational therapist may help a student with a pencil grip or letter formation while also helping them with paragraph writing within their general education classroom. A speech pathologist may help a student with articulation and learning science vocabulary terms while also facilitating social interactions through a group project during a science lesson.

Providing instruction to students in an alternate setting, done either one-to-one or in a small group, has a different set of benefits. An alternate setting provides a quieter, less distracting environment. Though the general education setting provides the opportunity for many positive interactions and experiences for students, it can also be difficult for students to focus, process, and think in a room with 25 other students and additional adults.

Focused, alternate-setting instruction provides content for students precisely at their current educational level. This method is often necessary if students are being provided with modified content. For example, if a student is reading multiple years below their grade level, it would be appropriate for that student to receive one-to-one or small group instruction. This instruction, which should include appropriate interventions such as a systematic multisensory reading curriculum, would occur at their current level in an attempt to close or narrow the gap for their reading. The ultimate goal is to close the instructional gap and reintroduce the student to the grade level curriculum in their general education environment.

Determining setting for students with specialized social–emotional needs

For students with specialized social–emotional needs, determining where instruction takes place is not always clear cut. Students with significant social and emotional needs present throughout the entire range of cognitive and academic abilities. A student with an emotional disability may have average to above-average cognitive ability and no additional disabilities. A student with an emotional disability may also have comorbidities such as a learning disability, autism, or a communication disability which increases their level of need in a school environment. The level of academic need plays a majority role in determining where a student will receive their academic services. However, a student's emotional disability can also play a significant role in the determination.

All students who qualify for special education services do so by having a disability that impacts their ability to access curriculum in school. These students are protected by a law called the Individuals with Disabilities Education Act, or IDEA. IDEA provides a free and appropriate public education (FAPE) to qualifying students with disabilities in the United States. IDEA requires that necessary special education and related services are provided to students (Wright & Wright, 2007, p. 45).

In 1975, the Education for All Handicapped Children Act, which later developed into IDEA, was signed into law. Through this law, students with disabilities who were formerly denied a public education were provided with FAPE through the LRE. The LRE for students clause states that students should be in a general education environment with their neurotypical and neurodivergent peers to the maximum extent that is *appropriate*. The word "appropriate" here leaves room for some subjectivity and additionally provides the need for an individualized approach to each student's day. Though two or more students may share the same general education classroom and therapeutic learning program, the amount of time that it is appropriate for a student to be in the general education environment with their peers will be different for each individual. Additionally, the most appropriate setting in a school community is partially dependent on what services the school district offers. If the district does not have an adequately appropriate learning program in-district, the district must pay tuition toward an out-of-district placement (Wright & Wright, 2007, pp. 72–74).

The goal for all students in a public school setting is to have as much inclusive time with their peers as possible in a general education setting. However, it is important to factor in a student's ability to access the curriculum as well as consider their emotional well-being throughout the course of the school day. Within a therapeutic inclusion program, there will never be a cookie-cutter, one-size-fits-all answer for the amount of time that students should spend in their program classroom versus their general education classroom. It must be determined for each student in regard to their academic presentation, as dictated by their IEP, and also by a student's daily presentation and ability to navigate their school day across general education and specialized environments.

Henry and Anthony's academic settings

Two second-grade boys, Henry and Anthony, are members of the Oak classroom as well as the same second-grade general education classroom. Both boys share some common interests such as superheroes, soccer, and technology. They also share some common challenges with impulsivity and occasional physical aggression and property destruction, which were among factors that led to their common placement in the Oak Program.

However, these boys are also very different in many ways. Henry has anxiety, as well as ADHD. His home life and schooling thus far have not had any significant known traumas, yet his disabilities make a typical school day very difficult for Henry to navigate. Henry also has average to superior cognitive abilities, and, with the right accommodations and supports in place, is able to access the second-grade general education curriculum.

Henry requires the assistance of a teacher or paraprofessional from the Oak Program in order to regulate his behavior and impulsivity in his general education classroom at all times. Though it took some time to get used to, and there was certainly resistance at first, Henry knows that the teachers from his program are there to support him throughout his day and to help him be successful. Staff from the Oak Program work with Henry's second-grade classroom teacher, Ms. Ng, to accommodate and integrate Henry within the classroom group. Henry has preferential seating, which allows him to focus on instruction. Oak staff also provide gentle prompting when Henry's attention begins to wander. Some days, this is all of the support that Henry requires to be successful during academic instruction in the general education environment.

Other days, however, Henry requires more support. The Oak Program is set up to provide Henry with the support that he needs, both on days when his need to access the supports of the program is minimal and on days when his needs are more intense. There are days when Henry cannot focus in the general education environment. His inability to focus is not only a detriment to his academic progress. When he cannot focus on academic work, he tends to shift his focus to social conflicts, which can lead to further complications. On these days, the Oak staff has the ability to work with Henry one-to-one in a quiet room. Before delving into the academics that are happening concurrently in the general education classroom, they are able to co-regulate with Henry as they seek an emotional state that will allow him to reengage with learning. Though Henry does require a placement alternative at some points in his education, as well as some accommodations, he does not require any modifications to his curriculum, receiving all of his academic instruction at grade level.

Though Anthony can appear to present similarly to Henry to those who do not know the boys well, they are actually quite different both in their backgrounds and current presentation. Anthony's story involves trauma. The history of trauma has provided him with a background that presents obstacles in his current emotional life that need to be overcome. Additionally, Anthony has a developmental delay. This delay has made the ability to learn to read extremely difficult for Anthony. Now that he is in second grade, most of Anthony's grade-level peers can read easy to moderate texts and read for both enjoyment and learning. Anthony is still learning to decode texts at a kindergarten level with a great amount of effort. Not only is the process of learning to read extremely difficult for Anthony, there is a large amount of shame that he puts on himself as he knows that he cannot perform as well as his peers.

As a result of his need for significant reading intervention, Anthony receives one-to-one reading instruction daily from his Oak special education teacher. This instruction is based in a systematic, sequential multisensory reading program. This happens in a quiet, calm setting where Anthony can both focus on the task at hand and receive reading content at his instructional level. Given Anthony's low self-esteem and perception of failure regarding his ability to read, the instruction does not look the same as it may for a student with a developmental delay or a language-based learning disability. Anthony requires an extremely thoughtful, scaffolded approach to his reading. He begins each reading block with a five-minute break which he uses to play with toys or draw. These are calming activities that put him in the right mindset for the hard work to come. Anthony is then presented with a visual checklist of his tasks for the day. He is able to reorder the tasks, and have a moderate amount of control over the reading session while still completing the designated tasks. He also has short breaks peppered throughout the session to provide momentum and allow him to put all of his effort forward knowing that there will be an endpoint in 10–15 minutes. Most days, Anthony is able to complete a 45–60-minute reading session within this framework.

Other days, Anthony becomes overwhelmed with his inability to read like his peers. On these days, Anthony often repeats phrases like "I'm so stupid," "I hate you," and "I can't do this." When this occurs, the focus on reading shifts to a focus on Anthony and his mental health. Providing Anthony with love, reassurance, and a calm presence to process his feelings are what he needs more than a lesson on decoding. When this happens, the lesson is picked up the following day, knowing that the academic learning cannot occur without addressing Anthony's self-esteem and mental health.

Though Anthony has significant difficulties with his reading, averaging about two years below grade level, other areas of his academic learning are on par with his peers. For most other subject areas, mathematics, writing, social studies, and science, Anthony is able to access grade-level curriculum alongside his peers. Though Anthony still requires special education services in order to access the math and writing curriculum with his general education peers, the general education environment with support from program staff is the best place for this instruction to occur. Support is provided by a special education teacher, or from other program staff with supervision and consultation from a special education teacher.

A flexible approach to setting determinations

In order to serve our students in the least restrictive environment, we take a subject-by-subject approach to each student's service delivery. Simply because a student has an inability to access one subject in the general education environment, it does not mean that student should receive all of their academics in a substantially separate environment.

Unfortunately, many models of special education programming for students with social–emotional needs do not have the flexibility that we are suggesting. Both private therapeutic schools and more rigid social–emotional programming within the public school environment do not have the capability to truly provide students with the least restrictive environment. These environments often have students receiving all of their academic instruction through their program in a pull-out model, out of the general education environment.

Anthony's academic settings continued

While Anthony is in the general education environment, he receives all of the same content as his peers. Though sometimes unintentional, instruction delivered in a substantially separate environment can lead to a watered-down curriculum. While it is sometimes necessary to provide modifications to the curriculum, this is not necessary for Anthony in regard to math instruction. Additionally, Anthony receives the input and discussion that his peers contribute in the classroom. In a general education classroom environment, students often ask questions that the teacher has not thought of, provide reteaching in student-friendly words, and provide peer-based support that is unavailable in a one-to-one or small group environment.

While many of his peers can attend to math instruction for an hour straight with their teacher, this is not the case for Anthony. Despite a general education teacher who provides enthusiastic and differentiated teaching, without support Anthony would not be consistently successful in this environment. This is where the staff in the Oak Program provide support that allows for success. In addition to the presence of Oak staff in the general education classroom, the Oak team maintains a close working relationship with the general education teacher in order to facilitate this level of support and flexibility from all of the adults working with Anthony.

While Anthony is in his general education classroom for math instruction, he often sits close to his general education teacher so that she can provide focus for him during the direct instruction of the lesson. Additionally, his Oak teacher is close by for two reasons. The Oak teacher can provide additional support to Anthony if he needs it, either by reteaching or reinforcing the curriculum, or by providing encouragement and mental health support. If the general education environment becomes too overwhelming, this staff member can aid Anthony in using strategies that he has learned in the Oak Program, such as engaging in breathing activities, utilizing scales such as the size of the problem, or taking a break. This staff member is also able to take Anthony from the general education classroom to a one-to-one environment to continue the lesson and curriculum for the day if he is unable to regulate and access the curriculum at that time.

Equally important, if Anthony is regulated, focused, and attending to the curriculum, the Oak teacher can help other students in the general education classroom to free his teacher, Ms. Ng, to help Anthony. Receiving help and guidance from his general education teacher as well as the Oak staff serves a variety of purposes, as covered in detail in Chapter Five. Primarily, fostering a relationship with Anthony's general education teacher shows him that he is truly a member of that classroom community.

When students can be integrated into the general education classroom successfully, there are two important pieces that add to the student's school experience. First, the student is able to feel, as students typically verbalize, "normal." While there is a huge variance of what is considered actually normal, or typical, for a public school experience from the viewpoint of administration, teachers, and special education staff, that does not often carry over to children. Children in the public school system in the United States really view normal as being in a classroom with a teacher and roughly 15 to 25 peers. Being able to support students with social and emotional disabilities to access their general education environments provides a feeling that they are not as different from their school peers as they may feel when educated in a completely substantially separate environment. Providing students and general education teachers the support to foster this relationship, through both successful and challenging moments in the classroom, is key.

In addition to a student's self-perception of having a "normal" school experience, taking part in the general education classroom allows them to practice developing social and self-regulation capacities in a less therapeutically specialized environment. In the general education classroom students navigate diverse peer relationships, classroom expectations, and general education teachers who cannot always be as tuned into the state of their mental health as the therapeutic inclusion program staff. The general education environment is often an ideal setting to practice social and self-regulation skills honed in the therapeutic program classroom. Program students are able to become a part of the social situations that all parents send their students to school to experience, but with the support of a team who can work through challenging situations when necessary.

Conclusion

Determining the academic setting and workload for a student in a therapeutic inclusion program is not a one-size-fits-all approach. In fact, it's the opposite. In order to determine what the day-to-day environment and curriculum will look like for each student in the therapeutic inclusion program, it is vital to take a student-by-student approach. By doing this, the students will truly be provided with the least restrictive environment, balancing academic rigor with the therapeutic milieu support that they need in order to be successful throughout the day. In order to accomplish this, a plan must be laid out for students. However, as the teacher, it is imperative to be willing and able to deviate from the plan based on a student's daily presentation and varying need for social and emotional support and guidance.

References

National Governors Association Center for Best Practices, Council of Chief State School. (2010). Development process. In *Common Core State Standards*. Retrieved July 9, 2021, from www.corestandards.org

Wright, P. W., & Wright, P. D. (2007). *Wrightslaw: Special Education Law* (2nd ed., pp. 45–74). Harbor House Law Press.

7 Working with Behavior

In therapeutic work we deeply engage with the emotional and social inner landscape of those that we serve. Behavior is the visible part of the student's emotional and social landscape. It is the part on the surface. Behavior connects to a much larger, subterranean and dynamic structure that includes thoughts, feelings, and interpersonal images (or object relations) (Segal, 1964).

In this framework behavior is only the tip of a much more significant structure. Nonetheless, behavior is directly important to student's social lives, as well as a major factor in their capacity to learn in groups. Regardless of what is happening internally, behavior is how other people experience the student. This creates a social–behavioral–emotional feedback loop. How students are experienced by others is of great importance to the student's own experience and sense of self.

Therapeutic work can be conceptualized as working inside-out, or outside-in. Inside-out work engages with feelings and thoughts through discussion, expression, play, and creativity. This influences the student's behavior, which is how they interact with the world and are experienced by others. For example, a break spent arranging a sand tray garden may reduce a student's anxiety and help them return to a work group ready to contribute positively through their behavior.

Outside-in work focuses on the practical and surface behavior issues. When students experience interpersonal success and emotional relief from changing behaviors, this can positively influence their thoughts and feelings, leading to lasting positive change over time in both their behavior and their inner emotional landscape. Behavior intervention plans are an outside-in approach.

Most often in the therapeutic inclusion program a reasonable balance of both inside-out and outside-in work is in progress with any given student.

This chapter describes the primacy of the relationship-based therapeutic approach in the therapeutic inclusion program. Within therapeutic relationships there is a place for effective behavior-based interventions. The therapeutic inclusion program's approach to creating behavioral interventions is discussed. Behavior plan rewards can be used to support the development of a social and playful program culture. Safety issues and responses are also discussed,

DOI: 10.4324/9781003270478-8

including de-escalation, restraint, seclusion, and the controversies that arise around significantly dangerous escalation and staff intervention. Many of these pieces are demonstrated in the vignette describing the ongoing development of behavior management and interventions in the program group.

Working with behavior in the therapeutic inclusion program

In considering behavior, it is important to again recognize that the therapeutic inclusion program is designed to work with students with significant social, emotional, and behavioral difficulties. While some students with significant behavior issues can respond very quickly to the program, more often the progress is incremental. No book or chapter on behavior, including the contents of this volume, contains approaches that work for all students with significant behavioral difficulties.

Books or programs that tout proprietary approaches make cases for their broad and successful application. The therapeutic inclusion program is different. The program has a relationship-based philosophy and does not otherwise rely on a specific approach to behavioral intervention. In this sense, the therapeutic inclusion program is a reliable container and creative space where a variety of interventions can be implemented.

In the therapeutic inclusion program, the relationship is the first part of behavior management. The staff should have an orientation toward generosity and flexibility, while being consistent and maintaining clear boundaries and limits. Many times consistency and flexibility are thought of as opposites. A more useful conceptual frame for the therapeutic inclusion program is to imagine consistency as a sturdy structure built through reliability. This structure provides the space and credibility necessary to be flexible and creative. In this way, consistency supports the capacity for flexibility.

Unconditional positive regard (Rogers, 1961) lays a foundation for the students to be successful. Fortunately, with appropriate support, helping students with significant social, emotional, and behavioral difficulties is a positive and exciting opportunity. From the beginning, the opportunity to help is so rich, it gives staff every reason to regard the students with hope and excitement.

Similarly, the new start for a student or school year in the program often feels alive with positive possibility. Like their peers throughout the school, therapeutic inclusion program groups usually start the school year hoping for the best in terms of their ability to succeed in the school framework. This "honeymoon" period shows the group what is possible.

The group dynamics become more complex as students settle in and differentiate from the honeymoon phase. Over time, most students demonstrate the challenges that required their placement in the therapeutic inclusion program. In parallel, the group develops habits and a community personality. Throughout, the staff continues to offer the students hope, in the form of continued belief in the students and positive regard.

Relationships first ...

Behaviorism asserts that behavior is the observable and measurable part of the human experience, and as such the only part that can be approached for adjustment (Skinner, 1974). Behaviorism progenitor John Watson put forward that observable behavior was all that was needed in order to understand and help people experiencing issues identified as psychological. Introspection, insight, and interpretation were impossible to measure and therefore unnecessary concepts for treatment. And furthermore, we do not need information beyond what is observable in order to modify behavior (Watson, 1913). As the field developed over the century, most behaviorists have more flexible ideas about the role of thoughts and feelings than those put forward by behaviorism's founders.

The therapeutic inclusion program rejects this viewpoint and seeks to understand aspects of the student's experience which cannot be directly observed. It is crucial to strive to know and understand each student, with a spirit of humility and compassion in the face of the often difficult effort. In the process of understanding and working together, the student will know themselves better as well.

It is crucial to understand that healing takes place not in a sterling moment of perfect understanding, but instead in the process of growing toward greater understanding. In this process the student can feel seen and known authentically, cared for and positively regarded throughout. One of the great anxieties of many students is the fear that if they are truly known they will not be cared for and loved.

... then consider behaviorism

The therapeutic inclusion program does seek to help students modify their behavior. Behaviorism is the field of psychology with a special focus and reservoir of expertise in behavior modification. In using behavioristic techniques, the therapeutic inclusion program supports approaches that fit within the relationship-based framework, with a preference for positive behavioral interventions.

Behaviorism seeks to identify a cause for an individual's behavior that will fall under one of the four categories of reinforcement: attention, escape, access, or automatic (Cipani & Schock, 2007). Once one or more of the reinforcers is identified, then a behaviorist will, typically, develop a behavior intervention plan to reduce maladaptive behaviors. There is a wide range of approaches to choose from when developing a behavior intervention plan. A behaviorist working in consultation with the therapeutic inclusion program will have room for creativity and individuality within determining behavioral interventions. The therapeutic classroom that develops, including the behavior management approach, will be a reflection of the needs and personality of the group.

The following are some concepts and approaches that can work well within the therapeutic inclusion program and therapeutic inclusion program classroom in terms of behavior management. These are best implemented initially in the therapeutic inclusion program classroom.

Behavior management of the classroom group in the general education classroom is primarily led by general education teachers, in consultation and collaboration with the therapeutic inclusion program. The teacher's behavior management approach with the general classroom group is the starting point at which we consider any individual accommodations that support therapeutic inclusion program students.

The importance of stop

When behaviors and emotional temperatures are escalating, the energy generated can take on the quality of a snowball collecting mass as it rolls down the mountain. These are the circumstances that can escalate to safety concerns. Before anything else happens, before any presented problems are approached, the group and individuals must learn to stop in order for interventions to have space to operate.

The flexibility to say "yes" is one of the great privileges of working with a small group in a therapeutic inclusion program. As educators our capacity to say "yes" or our need to say "no" are often dictated by the size of the group we are working with. The collective needs of a group of 25 students make it difficult to explore individual student's whims and ideas. In a group of seven, staff can often make space and time to be responsive to individual ideas, while tending to the group.

For students with a tendency to escalate behaviorally, learning to stop is of utmost importance. The therapeutic inclusion program should reinforce that stopping is rewarding. The program should demonstrate that the crisis-sense that can come over the student can be safely noted, and set aside to make room for thoughtful responses. How to achieve this will look different for various groups, stages of development, and individuals.

Calm corner

Students who will benefit from learning how to stop should be rewarded for stopping in the middle of a potential escalation. A calm corner is probably the first, best idea to try and introduce. A calm corner is a space in a classroom designed to be a relaxing space. While its design will depend on developmental levels and the individuals in the group, it may contain a beanbag, pillows, blankets, stuffed animals, and books.

The use of a calm corner, with guidance from a program staff member and incentive, can make potential escalation an opportunity for growth. The calm corner, and how to use it, can be introduced through a social story. Students who may benefit from using the calm corner should role-play with a staff member around an escalating situation and the use of the calm corner. This way, the heat of the moment will not be the first time the student has the experience of using it.

Stop chair

Depending on the students, their relational styles, and their developmental progress, some students may not be prepared for this cooperative approach to de-escalation and "stop." When escalated, some students have difficulty with the possibilities presented by the array of items in the calm corner. Not all students are developmentally ready to feel personally responsible about stopping. They may depend on an external authority to help hold this responsibility. These students may benefit from a simple chair to sit in, at the direction of staff. This might be called a stop chair, a time-out chair, or a calm down chair.

The stopping spot should be in the therapeutic inclusion program classroom so that the student does not feel ostracized from the group. The staff should be clear that this is a place to calm down and stop, and that the student can do a great job stopping. In the interest of normalizing each student getting what they need, this can and should be non-stigmatizing. The staff should not establish a stopping place outside the group as the norm, as it suggests that student's difficulties with stopping and their big emotions are not acceptable. However, if an individual student prefers a private place to stop, that should be respectfully provided.

The aim is to help the student develop the capacity to stop on their own, eventually including stopping in the place they happen to be. However, the students who have the ability to do this are generally not the students who need extra support and structure with de-escalation. Usually, the intermediary step of a special stopping place is necessary, be it the collaborative style of the calm corner or something staff directed like time out.

This intervention is useful for some students in instances of verbal aggression, threats of violence, and physical aggression, that significantly disrupt the sense of safety in the therapeutic program classroom. A visual timer such as the Time Timer® is an important tool in supporting students in de-escalation and stopping. Making sure the student has an understanding of when it will be time to check in is very helpful, regardless of the approach.

Picking a time between three to five minutes is often effective. The goal is to be able to simply stop and sit for the period of time. For some students a blanket or fidget may help, but for others it can be hard to manage an object while de-escalating. The period of time can be reset if the student is unable to stop.

When the student is able to stop for the period of time, the process can end with a (often short) conversation. Since using a stopping chair is usually staff-directed, it is ethical and helpful for the student to be informed about why the teacher decided to use the stopping chair. Avoid expectations that the student agree with the staff member's perspective on what occurred, and avoid expectations of apologies. It is absolutely fine for the student to have their own and different perspective about what happened. These differing perspectives may or may not be resolved at some point, but this moment is not the time. Since staff-directed use of a stopping chair is often used in response to safety concerns, it is often necessary for maintaining safety that the student agree not to repeat the behavior in order to move on.

Behavior intervention plans

Behavior intervention plans are tools used to help a student adjust their habituated responses. Behavior intervention plans are now fundamental tools in school counseling and special education, and general education teachers are also now mostly familiar with them. A BCBA will be an expert resource for behavior intervention plan development.

For the purposes of the therapeutic inclusion program there are some aspects of quality behavior intervention plans and their implementation worth emphasizing.

At the introduction to the plan, the child should be invited into the plan in a respectful and thoughtful way. As always, the thoughtful consideration of the unique individual student is a central feature of the program.

Behavior intervention plan design considerations

Imagine a student who would benefit from remembering to take a break and cool down when frustrated, or a student who plays too rough at recess. These kinds of habits take root. In the moment of difficulty, it is hard for the student to remember they have other options. The maladaptive reaction becomes mostly automatic, even though it reliably leads to increased frustration and distress. With some external help in the form of a plan, a reward, and a supportive staff member, the student has a great opportunity to feel more successful and avoid the repetitive distress.

Behavior intervention plans are a creative undertaking. There is no limit to the aspects and features to consider.

Given that establishing a therapeutic relationship is foundational in the therapeutic inclusion program, there are three other key aspects to highlight for plans to be successful in the program.

First is student buy-in. The child should be motivated by the reward and understand why the behavior change they are working on will decrease their distress.

Second, the plan should be as simple as possible. At every step in plan design, from choosing a target behavior, to monitoring, data tracking, and reward delivery, simplicity should always be kept high priority. Small inefficiencies create exponential burdens over time and can result in a high cost in how well the plan is carried out. Through behavior intervention plans the staff is asking the student to change a deeply ingrained behavior. Changing these types of habits requires a major effort. In order for the student to stick with this difficult undertaking, the staff must maintain very high credibility in carrying out the plan with fidelity. If the staff starts to flag, the student sees this and it becomes very hard for the student to maintain the intense effort required to change a habituated response.

Third, the plan should be positively reinforced as much as possible. In most cases, it is possible for the plan to be solely based on earning reward. It is important to keep in mind that even when the plan is entirely based on earning the student is likely to experience difficult feelings of loss. There are two reasons for this. Though the reward is initially a new and exciting addition, failing to earn a valued reward can be experienced as a loss. Additionally, the maladaptive behavior we are helping the student change is on a deep level of great value to them. At some point in their development, it served them well. Even though the behavior may cause the student significant distress, asking them to stop a behavior is similar to asking for them to say goodbye to a special blanket, or a favorite stuffed animal. The staff should be prepared for the student to have strong feelings about this.

A purely positive plan should be the first effort and usually is the best design. However, some students will not progress without a sense of containment from both the positive and negative sides of the consequence spectrum. That being said, there should never be a plan for a student to lose access to something students regularly have access to as part of a behavior intervention plan. For example, a student should never lose access to recess with their peers as part of their behavior intervention plan.

A scale can be an effective way to implement positive and negative consequences when needed, without the potential loss of something students normally have access to. Sometimes a scale is called a "clip up clip down chart" (see Figure 7.1). In this plan, moving up is a positive consequence and represents moving toward the reward, and moving down is the negative consequence, moving away from the reward. Some educators associate clip up clip down charts with an approach where the chart is posted on the wall of the classroom. We are not recommending that. The scale we are describing is individual and private.

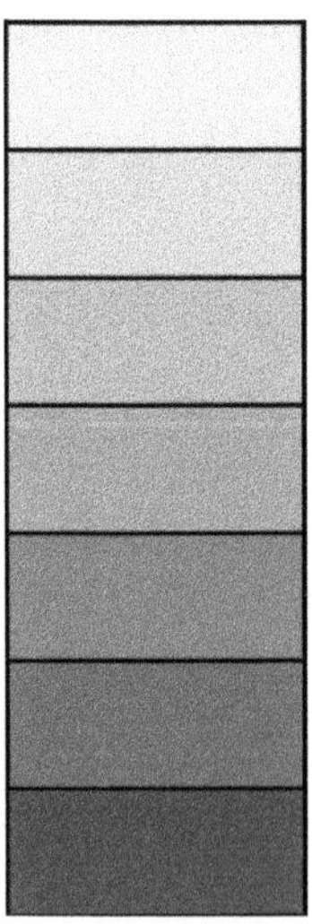

Figure 7.1 "Clip up clip down" chart. Image by Benjamin Murray.

The reward must be something special and separate from the expected daily experience of their peers. In comparison to their peers, the student is doing extra work in changing ingrained habits, and very difficult work at that. An extra reward is appropriate.

Social rewards

The therapeutic inclusion program is intended to create a fun and rewarding social group for students who have had difficulty being in groups. Many therapeutic inclusion program students have had limited or no experience enjoying the comforting and fun flow of a group that is functioning well.

One of the best ways to cultivate this culture is by rewarding students with appealing and social rewards. Depending on developmental stages and interests this can include access to special toys that the students can play with together. This can include building toys such as LEGO®, games, sports activities, art activities, and music activities.

When student interests and reward times can be coordinated, it creates positive momentum for a good social time together. The students arrive to reward time feeling positive about having earned their reward. The positivity follows into their play, creating a golden opportunity for positive group development.

Given that therapeutic inclusion program students need practice and experience feeling good and successful in groups, it is best to develop a classroom culture that emphasizes person-to-person connections and deemphasizes technology. Technology-based rewards, such as games on a computer screen, are often appealing to students. But they are also often isolating and usually do not provide the kind of development of group cohesion and mood lift that quality social play offers.

Introducing behavior intervention plans to students

In most cases, behavior intervention plans should be introduced to the student in a group format, with the rest of the program members. This would generally take place during morning circle or meeting. Normalizing behavior intervention plans in the group is another way of communicating and validating the students as individuals who are working on different things. The students get the message that while they may be working on different goals, they are not alone in their effort to grow and work on things that can be difficult. Their universality and individuality can both be validated this way.

An age-appropriate social story (Gray, 2015) can support the introduction of a behavior intervention plan. This is especially true for elementary school students, and for students relatively new to the program or at the beginning of the school year. For older students the key features of a social story, the previewing and step-by-step understanding centered on the experience of the student, can be delivered in developmentally appropriate ways such as a conversation with some notes, illustrations, or diagrams.

Interpersonally, the behavior intervention plan should be offered authentically as something that is designed "to help you with something that has been difficult." The maladaptive habits that make it difficult to be a member of the group are almost always sources of distress for the student. Students love to feel successful at school and valued by their peers. For most students in the therapeutic inclusion program, unlearning maladaptive responses and habituating new responses is part of the process of getting there.

Responding to safety needs

Because the therapeutic inclusion program will serve students with significant behavioral difficulties, sometimes practical modifications to student's plans will become necessary due to safety concerns. For example, if a student is hitting and kicking other students at recess, a special plan will be necessary in order to keep students safe, as well as protecting the student from stigmatization that can come along with making others feel unsafe. This student may need a special recess plan. A plan might include having a staff member nearby throughout recess, or doing a separate activity with a staff member, intended to meet some of the same needs of play and movement.

Alongside behavioral intervention plans, it should be clear to the student that practical modifications to maintain safety are not part of any behavior intervention plan. Despite their intention, changes to student plans in order to maintain safety are likely to evoke emotional responses from students. These feelings should be heard respectfully just like any other feelings the students may share.

De-escalation and restraint

In descriptions and trainings de-escalation is always paired with restraint, in order to emphasize that verbal and nonverbal de-escalation is always preferable to intervening physically. The therapeutic inclusion program is built around de-escalation. Every aspect of the milieu classroom is designed to help students feel safe, secure, connected, and listened to, with the aim of avoiding escalation.

A 2013 Massachusetts report on out-of-district placements (Hehir et al., 2013) found that the majority of students in Massachusetts were receiving out-of-district placements due to safety concerns. While further data on this question is sparse, it is known that safety concerns drive a significant number of out-of-district placements to specialized schools.

Over time, with a population of students with very significant behavioral issues that would otherwise lead to out-of-district placements, there are likely to be instances where physical intervention and restraint occur. Even the most skilled and experienced de-escalators cannot avoid the need for physical intervention in every instance.

The term "physical intervention" is sometimes used here because the way most people envision "restraint" or "seclusion" does not encompass the range of how it actually appears.

The federal restraint and seclusion guidelines define restraint to include an intervention that "reduces the ability of a student to move his torso, arms, legs, or head freely" (Federal Department of Education, 2012). Combined with the important and common sense rule that staff should use minimal necessary force to ensure safety, minimal physical interventions often qualify as restraint. For example, imagine a staff member noticing a deeply angry first grader about to attack another first grader. Many staff members might put their body in between the students. The student, in a rage and aiming for their peer, instead runs into the barrier of the staff member's legs. The staff member remains there in order to protect the other student, while the first grader pushes against the staff member's legs. The staff member has reduced the ability of the student to move freely and is engaged in a physical restraint according to federal guidelines and most state-level regulations. Many events that qualify as physical restraints look more like this minimal intervention, rather than a more immobilizing restraint that is usually associated with the word.

In the field, the frequency with which these physical interventions are reported as restraints in accordance with regulations is unclear. Programs should carefully follow the letter of the law, despite the tendency of districts to pressure programs to find rationales for not classifying physical interventions as restraints. This tendency to seek a way to dismiss what may appear to be inconsequential physical interventions is driven by the desire of administrators to avoid the scrutiny that restraints bring. However, this scrutiny is important in order to safeguard children and staff.

The most faithful efforts to apply federal and state guidelines in real-world situations are confounded, due to the lack of coherence of the laws themselves. Laws, regulations, and policies can only be improved to the benefit of our students and staff when direct service providers and administrators insist on accurate reporting, giving policy-makers the information they need.

As laws, regulations, and practices currently stand, the staff who directly encounter dangerous situations are vulnerable due to the vagaries of the law. Administrations, in consultation with experienced experts, must create and communicate a clear and consistent interpretation of the laws that govern restraint and seclusion for their school district.

The controversy around management of escalated and physically dangerous situations

If part of the school district's intention in establishing a therapeutic inclusion program is reducing out-of-district placements, then the district must seriously consider whether it is prepared to deal with the distress that can arise when restraint and seclusion are needed.

Physical restraint is a topic that stirs anxiety and strong feelings among people. There are serious, documented, and well-known problems that stem from physical restraint in schools. These include institutions and instances where restraint has been used irresponsibly and abusively (Abamu, 2019). At the same time, there are serious and documented problems with students hurting peers (Turanovic & Siennick, 2022) and staff (Longobardi et al., 2019).

A well-supported, staffed, and supervised therapeutic inclusion program does not always prevent serious escalation. The root source of the distress which can lead to a student physically and dangerously acting out is their deep emotional pain and anguish. It is the therapeutic inclusion program's design to help alleviate this distress. The very understandable wish that this deep distress did not exist at all, accompanies the wish that physical intervention was never necessary to ensure safety.

Unfortunately, the anguish that some students experience due to a variety of reasons, and leads them to act out unsafely, is very real. There are a number of organizations working to reduce and eliminate restraint and seclusion, doing excellent work. Some, such as the Alliance Against Seclusion and Restraint, make suggestions aligned with the relationship-based philosophy we describe for the therapeutic inclusion program (Stephens, 2022). A relationship-based approach, flexibility, nonjudgmental attunement, and a thoughtful respect to the issues as seen by the student will go a long way to prevent escalation. However, they cannot on their own reliably prevent serious injury in the moment that a student is experiencing a difficult and dangerous episode.

Physical intervention is necessary when a student is otherwise likely to seriously injure themselves or others. It must always be done using the least force required to maintain safety. When a student is likely to seriously injure themselves or others without physical intervention, the staff that is physically intervening has two fundamental ways to prevent injury: (1) Restraint: a minimally necessary reduction in freedom of mobility in which the student is prevented from hurting himself or others. (2) Seclusion: a specialized room where the student can be alone until the safety risk decreases. Unless the student is already in a room that could be used for seclusion, seclusion often requires a transport to the room where the seclusion will occur. This transport usually requires a restraint as defined by restraint regulations, because in most instances a student acting out unsafely will not voluntarily enter a seclusion room.

The current state of laws and regulations

In the United States, the federal government offers guidelines on restraint and seclusion (Federal Department of Education, 2012). Each state has their own laws and regulations. Many state's regulations regarding restraint are less than coherent and difficult to apply to real-world situations. Most states in some way reflect the federal guidance that physical intervention should only be used when there is an "imminent threat of serious physical harm" (Federal Department of Education, 2012, p. 2). Though, what constitutes serious physical harm, and determining whether it is imminent, leaves the door open to different interpretations.

Given the subjective and sometimes contradictory nature of restraint and seclusion laws and regulations, there is a range of reasonable and defensible interpretations and applications of the laws. School districts usually partner with outside agencies to ensure that some staff members are trained in de-escalation and restraint.

In concert with their outside partner and de-escalation and restraint program, the district must have a clear understanding of their approach to physical intervention. This shared understanding must run from the school board, to the superintendent, to the special education director, down through administrative layers, to the staff of the therapeutic inclusion program. Students and parents of students who may require physical intervention should also understand the circumstances when a staff member may physically intervene. Furthermore, the district's interpretation and application should be the subject of ongoing evaluation.

If this level of shared understanding and communication is not in place, the therapeutic inclusion program and district may not be able to contain and process the distress associated with serious safety risks which can result in restraint and seclusion. The program may cease to be able to function under the stress. A safety situation featuring an imminent risk of serious physical harm does not guarantee that a parent, who is not present at school, understands or supports a restraint or seclusion.

Program flexibility, culture, and planning

As noted earlier in this chapter, the therapeutic inclusion program is not a rigidly prescribed set of interventions and responses. The therapeutic inclusion program is a structure and collection of core philosophies in which a range of educational and therapeutic interventions can be implemented.

This flexibility is important due to the unpredictable range of individual and group needs. The therapeutic inclusion program seeks to develop a sophisticated understanding of each student, which leads to increasingly individualized responsive care. The staff members bring their unique personalities, strengths, and weaknesses into the group as well. Adding to these factors, we have the physical resources of the school and the therapeutic inclusion program classroom, as well as the culture of the school. With so many variables, it would be foolish and counterproductive to prescribe a rigid set of responses. The program staff uses the therapeutic program model, through collaboration and supervision, to develop the evolving classroom culture, educational interventions, and therapeutic interventions that the group calls for, with the unique staff and physical resources at hand.

It is worth keeping in mind that there are many approaches and interventions that can help. The staff must pay close attention to choosing, implementing, and adjusting approaches and interventions. With so much close care and attention, it can be tempting to imagine that landing on a specific "best" approach is of utmost importance. Ironically, the care, consideration, and thoughtfulness that goes into program plans are actually the most important therapeutic elements at work. The thoughtful design and calibration that goes into student plans make them, most significantly, a conduit for this care and personal consideration.

Working with behavior in the Oak group

The members of the Oak Program group were introduced in Chapter Three. Their experience in the therapeutic inclusion program exemplifies how behavior intervention plans can develop and serve the unique needs of students and groups.

After about two weeks of the new group settling in at the beginning of the school year, behavior plans began to emerge. Nicole had done some individual work with the program counselor at the end of the previous year. They had used a behavior intervention plan structured around replacing her habit of yelling out disruptively during class with other behaviors such as doodling or taking a short structured break.

As Nicole started first grade, she joined the therapeutic inclusion program. Nicole's former maladaptive behavior of yelling out disruptively did not travel with her to first grade. She continued to utilize the strategies that she had learned in kindergarten to replace this behavior. However, Nicole was not completing her classwork without crying, and ripping or throwing her papers. The staff developed a plan where tasks were broken down into three elements. Nicole was rewarded for completion of the three steps with a tally mark. The tally marks were totaled and exchanged for time to play with special toys twice a day. This increased her ability to complete her schoolwork productively.

Amir, also in first grade, used a similar system. Additionally, in collaboration with his parents, a plan was developed where he could earn a single m&m® for using a stopping chair instead of tantruming. This plan was highly effective, and over time he transitioned to taking time in a stopping chair when upset without the m&m® incentive. He preferred to use a stopping chair alone in the small, multipurpose room adjacent to the therapeutic program classroom.

Anthony and Henry were in second grade. Their general education teacher, Ms. Ricci, used a "clip up clip down" system for the entire class. The system was a seven-step scale, and they began each day in the middle at step four. Ms. Ricci implemented this whole class behavior plan in a way that emphasized positive reinforcement. Most importantly, Anthony and Henry responded well to it.

The aim was to keep their behavior plans simple. This helps the students more easily integrate the plans into their thinking and keeps plans streamlined for consistent implementation. To this end, Ms. Ricci's clip up clip down system was used throughout the day, not only when students were in the general education environment. Like their classmates, the students could earn toward a prize box reward in Ms. Ricci's class by ending their time with her at the top of their charts. Additionally, they could earn a LEGO® playtime for reaching their clip up clip down chart goal at the end of each day with the Oak Program staff. Given Henry's extreme impulsivity, his goal was to end the day at a five on the scale, while Anthony's goal was to end the day at seven.

As months went on, plans evolved toward similarity, and then differentiated again. The clip up clip down charts were popular with the Oak group. Perhaps this was because it was a simple system and it was easy for the students to track their own progress and know what to expect. They also provided a flexible system that staff could apply to the individual behavioral needs of each student. For a time they were in use for all five students, clipping up and down based on their specific behavioral needs.

Meanwhile, the end of the day LEGO® play time was becoming increasingly valued by the group due to the positive social connections developing. Granted, staff had to provide close assistance in order to help maintain an experience that was social and fun most of the time, and there were plenty of instances where the group functioning took a difficult turn. But mostly, the children enjoyed playing together and cherished the time.

The social success during LEGO® reward time also had another important effect in strengthening group cohesiveness. The sense that they were a group that could play together, and enjoy each other, helped throughout the day. Play is an enjoyable, imaginative improvisation, and doesn't only occur during prescribed playtime. Play can occur in a fun conversation during morning meeting, during a funny attempt to go through a doorway simultaneously, or just about any time. In order to play together, the individuals need to be open to the improvisations of their play partners. This requires some trust building. Once that ability to trust and play is established, the ability to play together can infuse the group with the positive feelings that follow throughout the day. LEGO® reward played a significant part in the Oak group building trust.

The play also informs and facilitates the therapeutic work. In *Playing and Reality* (1971) D.W. Winnicott explained,

> Psychotherapy has to do with two people playing together. The corollary of this is that where playing is not possible then the work done by the therapist is directed towards bringing the patient from a state of not being able to play into a state of being able to play.
>
> (p. 38)

While the play itself is therapeutic, it also prepares the group for playing with ideas, ways of thinking, and perspectives during group psychotherapy and other conversations. Play bridges what is occurring to what is possible, between reality and fantasy. This is necessary in order to envision change.

In parallel with group development, behavior intervention plans and the reward time play evolved over time. Aida was a studious and well-behaved third grader, and always ended her day at the top of her clip up clip down chart. By December, her plan became obsolete. It was understood that she would earn the group playtime every day, and didn't need the chart. Aida needed the therapeutic inclusion program in order to develop social skills and receive support around intense and distressing emotional episodes, but behavior was not a special concern for her by this point.

A few months later, Anthony also had a feeling that he was outgrowing the clip up clip down chart. Anthony did continue to need behavioral support from a program staff member, but was nearly always finishing the day at the top of his chart, and felt that he wanted something different and more challenging. The program leaders saw this as a great opportunity for Anthony to be even more invested in his own growth. Anthony and the program co-leader Mrs. Tabor co-designed a new plan earning "stars," which were recorded in a small notebook. In this way, Anthony and Mrs. Tabor created a plan that was more challenging and offered an opportunity for more granular attention to parts of his day.

As the culture of the group and behavioral plans evolved, so did the reward time. After many months of enjoying LEGO® at the end of the day, the group started to take interest in some other toys and activities, particularly superhero action figures. The action figure play then evolved toward the students using math manipulatives to run a pretend restaurant for the staff. The staff used this to foster cooperative pretend play, acquiring a toy cash register and a set of play food. Soon this fun and comically unpredictable restaurant was taking orders, enlisting customers to work in the kitchen, negotiating roles, and dealing with a stream of customers in the form of the staff and students playing various roles.

An effective behavior intervention plan is calibrated so that the student should earn the reward most of the time. This supports positive feelings around growth and change and helps to sustain motivation. The Oak Program's plans were designed and adjusted with this in mind. However, given a group of five over a long number of days it was not very unusual on any given day for one or two students to not earn the reward. While sticking to the behavior plan, it is important to be compassionate to the students who do not earn their reward. Their feelings of disappointment are very understandable. Under these circumstances, students who did not meet their goals could read or draw at their desks while others had reward time. When it was hard for students to be in the same room as the play without being able to join, program staff supported them by offering the adjacent multipurpose room for some quiet space to read or draw.

Conclusion

The therapeutic inclusion program is designed to support students in maturing toward health in their thoughts, feelings, and behavior. It is a whole child approach. Thoughts and feelings are the largely invisible foundations on which behavior rests. While thoughts and feelings are not entirely knowable—often not even to the person experiencing them—it is a productive therapeutic process to seek to empathetically understand a student. When this is done in collaboration with the student, the student is invited toward mature self-understanding.

Feelings, thoughts, and behavior—each is significant, and each influences the others. Behavior, as the visible realm, is how we interact with others. This makes behavior central in the individual's efforts to feel successful in group settings. Behavior is also the realm where most individuals have the greatest degree of control. A behavior-focused approach can be effective for some students.

However, students appropriate for the therapeutic inclusion program have generally already found behavior-focused approaches to be insufficiently effective. The therapeutic program provides a relationship-based approach. In this secure structure, efforts toward deeper understanding are underway, and behavior modification techniques are implemented alongside efforts to better understand thoughts and feelings.

There are many elements that make up a therapeutic inclusion program. The program staff must respond to the unique and evolving needs of the student group presented. The staff responds with the personal set of resources they bring to the group, the contributions the students bring, the resources of the school, and in relationship to the school culture. It is easy to see that every therapeutic inclusion program will, and must be, unique.

The core philosophies and structure of the therapeutic inclusion program guide its development. This is analogous to the therapist/patient relationship in psychodynamic work. Every therapist/patient relationship is unique. The therapist's work is guided by therapeutic principles, and the therapist consults with their supervisor to guide them toward their best work. Neither the therapist nor the patient knows at the beginning exactly how the work will develop and what might be needed. Often, the sense of breakthrough with a student or group in the therapeutic inclusion programs arises when novel approaches and interventions are created. The therapeutic inclusion program is a structure that facilitates the invention of new approaches based on well-grounded therapeutic theory, the specific individuals involved, and the narratives in development.

If part of the intention of the program is to reduce out-of-district placements, the district and program should be prepared for safety concerns that can arise when caring for students with significant social, emotional, and behavioral difficulties. The staff must be well trained in de-escalation and restraint. All levels of the district administration must have a fundamental shared understanding of the training and application, in order to be prepared for the distress that can arise around safety concerns, de-escalation, and restraint.

References

Abamu, J. (2019). *How some schools restrain or seclude students: A look at a controversial practice*. NPR. www.npr.org/2019/06/15/729955321/how-some-schools-restrain-or-seclude-students-a-look-at-a-controversial-practice

Cipani, E., & Schock, K. M. (2007). Basic concepts and principles. In Cipani, E., & Schock, K. M. (Eds.), *Functional behavioral assessment, diagnosis, and treatment: A complete system for education and mental health settings* (pp. 1–17). Springer Publishing Company.

Gray, C. (2015). *The new social story book*. Future Horizons.

Hehir, T., Grindal, T., Ng, M., Schifter, L., Eidelman, H., & Dougherty, S. (2013, October). *Use of out-of-district programs by Massachusetts students with disabilities*. Massachusetts Departments of Elementary and Secondary Education. www.doe.mass.edu/sped/hehir/2013-10OutofDistrict.docx

Longobardi, C., Badenes-Ribera, L., Fabris, M. A., Martinez, A., & McMahon, S. D. (2019). Prevalence of student violence against teachers: A meta-analysis. *Psychology of Violence*, 9(6), 596–610.

Rogers, C. (1961). *On becoming a person*. Houghton Mifflin Company.

Segal, H. (1964). *Introduction to the work of Melanie Klein*. Basic Books.

Skinner, B. G. (1974). *About behaviorism*. Vintage Books.

Stephens, G. (2022, May 29). *If not seclusion and restraint then what do we do?*. Alliance Against Seclusion and Restraint. https://endseclusion.org/2022/05/29/if-not-seclusion-and-restraint-then-what-do-we-do/

Turanovic, J. J., & Siennick, S. E. (2022) *The causes and consequences of school violence: A review*. U.S. Department of Justice Office of Justice Programs. www.ojp.gov/pdffiles1/nij/302346.pdf

U.S. Department of Education. (2012). *Restraint and seclusion: Resource document*. U.S. Department of Education. www2.ed.gov/policy/seclusion/restraints-and-seclusion-resources.pdf

Watson, J. B. (1913). Psychology as the behaviorist views it. *Psychological Review*, 20(2), 158–177.

Winnicott, D. W. (1971). *Playing and reality*. Routledge.

8 Working with Parents and Guardians

The therapeutic inclusion program's work cannot be sustained without parent work and collaboration. Children with significant social, emotional, and behavioral difficulty, and their families require home–school partnerships, as these are the student's primary environments. Through continuous and collaborative work and communication, the environments of home and school are sewn together, forming a seam. The goal is for the home–school partnership to develop into connected environments that facilitate healthy growth.

This is what Winnicott called the "facilitating environment" (1965). This collaboration of program staff and parents fosters the safe and supportive environment that can hold the inevitable reactions to change. This chapter also describes the mechanics of parent communication and collaboration in the therapeutic inclusion program, as well as an approach toward confidentiality. A narrative from our work in the field demonstrates the therapeutic inclusion program's relationship-based approach to parent work and collaboration. In the narrative, the persistent and thoughtful collaboration between counselor and parent connects the student's two primary environments, allowing them to feel safe enough to abandon maladaptations and experiment with more sophisticated social and emotional responses.

Continuing with the metaphor of the seam, two pieces of fabric sewn together retain their unique qualities. No matter how tight the seam is sewn, the two pieces will not become a single piece of fabric, nor would that be desirable. Instead, the thread passes back and forth between the two, holding them together.

In the therapeutic inclusion program, the two pieces of fabric are home and school. The thread is the communication passing back and forth between the parent and the program. The goal is to create a tight enough seam for the child to experience feeling held securely. Naturally, as the child tests the security of their environment, they often push at this seam.

Maturation is not a journey of continuous progress, especially for children with significant social, emotional, and behavioral challenges. As they mature, children experience an internal conflict between their desire for autonomy and their desire to have all their needs taken care of by others. Daniel Siegel and Mary Hartzell (2014) call this "the tension between connection and autonomy" (p. 242).

DOI: 10.4324/9781003270478-9

Home–school communication and the student's conscious and unconscious responses

In considering communication between home and school and its impact on the development of the students in the therapeutic inclusion program, it is important to revisit the conceptual frameworks we use to understand the social, emotional, and behavioral development of the student. One's response to their environment are significant elements of their well-being and behavior. The therapeutic inclusion program aims to develop a care environment between home and school that facilitates maturation (Winnicott, 1965).

Chapter Seven describes behavior as the visible part of the child's experience, connected and directed by an expansive and less visible realm of thoughts and feelings. Our external environment acts on us as well, in ways that we are conscious of and in ways that usually go unrecognized. Children are especially responsive to their environments and do not have an adult capacity for self-regulation and metacognition.

In speaking to the impact of the relationship between home and school, this chapter references the conscious and unconscious motivations of the program's students. As a therapeutic inclusion program based on psychodynamic principles, it is important to recognize and discuss unconscious motivations. Often parent and general education teachers have some initial difficulty and confusion in the discussion of unconscious motivations of children. When discussing what motivates the child, they often wonder, "are they doing it on purpose?"

Resistance/fear of change

While there are exceptions, for most students home and school cohesion testing is driven by unconscious motivation. In these instances, the student does not have an understanding of what is driving their own behavior. As program staff considers and plans responses, it is not important nor possible to absolutely determine whether an understanding of the motivations behind the behavior is "true." What is important is determining whether program responses are providing relief to the student.

In an example of testing the cohesion of home and school working together, imagine a student hiding written communications from school to home that they know contain positive reports. The program can respond to the understanding that the student is testing the seam between home and school. The program, along with the student's parents, would reassure the student that "home and school work together" (Reinstein, 2006, p. 50), and that the student's therapeutic educators and parents communicate copiously about big things and little things, all in order to take the best care of the student. A personalized social story (Gray, 2015) is another excellent way to communicate this message. Once these messages are conveyed, the program staff and the parents can observe whether this response appears to provide relief and reassurance to the student.

Challenging behavior can be driven by the child's need to test whether they are seen and securely cared for. In becoming part of the therapeutic inclusion program, the students understand that they are part of something that is new to them. Most students understand that the program is designed to help care for them. But, crucial questions remain: "Can it care for me? Can it meet my needs?" Testing behavior is often how students attempt to answer these questions. As they test this new collaboration between home and school, the child can play hide and seek. While some familiar mischievous glee may be observed in this activity, as Winnicott observed (1965) "It is joy to be hidden but disaster not to be found" (p. 186).

We have all encountered fear of change, described in psychological terms as resistance (Freud & Breuer, 1895/1955). Oftentimes, the adaptations our students have developed in order to manage their social/emotional difficulties have served them well in formative experiences. These adaptations are often the same behaviors that now appear to stand in the way of social/emotional and academic functioning. In order to understand resistance, we must recognize that these behaviors/adaptations are tightly held and highly valued. An adaptation that was once a life preserver becomes a debilitating bind as the child grows within. Despite the resulting repeated distress and difficulty, on a deep level the child still regards the adaptation as a life preserver.

For example, a young child may experience conflict as the most reliable way to win their parent's undivided attention, an adaptation that may win them needed attention during a difficult period for their family where parental attention is pulled elsewhere. Past this difficult period, the behavioral pattern can remain within the family system. Later, the student carries this way of seeking security from their caretakers into the school environment. When the student is anxious they seek conflicts in order to secure teacher attention. The student may have a difficult time adjusting to new ways to feel secure among peers and caretakers, despite repetitive distress enacted by their habitual means of seeking security.

When the child senses the comprehensive containment of an effective home and school connection, conflicting feelings are often activated. The child is comforted by the cohesion, feeling increasingly seen, understood, and responsively cared for. At the same time there is a felt sense that this caring and cohesive system is an environmental change that may call for a different personal response. In other words, personal change may be called for. This fear of potential change drives the child to test the seam of the home/school connection.

As Daniel Reinstein describes in *To Hold and Be Held* students may respond by testing their ability to split home and school (2006). This can be done in a number of ways, including sharing conflicting versions of events between home and school, or trying to control what is communicated between environments. The therapeutic inclusion program uses these attempts to split as opportunities to demonstrate the home–school partnership.

Students do not tend to engage in splitting behavior in a consistent or continuous way. The student contains conflicting impulses, one moment reveling and thriving in the secure holding environment of the therapeutic inclusion program's collaboration with home, the next seeking to test its strength, and perhaps preserve cherished adaptations.

Home–school collaboration

The special education process, particularly via the development of an IEP, was created to facilitate a collaboration between home and school in the design of the student's program. A student's membership in a therapeutic inclusion program extends this collaboration. Beyond the IEP process (which is designed to facilitate periodic collaboration), the therapeutic inclusion program maintains an ongoing collaboration between program staff and parents.

In most cases parents arrive to the collaboration with the rich, lived experience of their child's development. Their contributions are invaluable in terms of informing the staff approach, designing effective interventions, and helping to understand what is transpiring within the school environment. These are the first and most directly observable layers of collaborative benefit.

Equally valuable is the way home–school collaboration imbues the care in both environments with an integrated sense of mutual respect and appreciation. An authentic collaboration with parents, supported by the therapeutic approach of the program co-leader, creates conditions that facilitate growth toward maturity for the student, as well as a home–school partnership that can contain and withstand distress.

The parent brings their deep experience to the collaboration. The program co-leader meets them with their professional knowledge, experience, and a fresh pair of eyes. Each bring different and meaningful value to the shared work.

Parent communication and confidentiality

People under 18 years of age do not have confidentiality rights in any comparable sense to an adult. While there are exceptions, generally speaking the child's parent are the holder of their child's confidentiality rights. For example, it is the parent's signature that is needed for a release of information to a third party.

Managing therapeutic confidentiality within a public school requires staff to clearly understand the boundaries of the therapeutic program. The therapeutic inclusion program staff, and the program supervisor, are the individuals within the confidentiality bubble. All confidential information from the therapeutic work with students and their families will be shared within the program staff bubble and will not be shared outside of it. This allows the staff to work in an informed and integrated fashion, while respecting the privacy of students and families. These confidentiality distinctions should be clearly communicated to students and their parent.

Because parent communication is an element of the therapeutic work for the students, parent communications are confidential. This means that the program staff cannot share communications with anyone outside the therapeutic inclusion program. This generally applies to the communication book and to the weekly parent conversation. However, there is discretion for the program staff to make distinctions between therapeutic content and practical issues such as scheduling and logistics that may need to be shared with staff outside the program, as comes up in any educational or care setting.

The therapeutic inclusion program, while maintaining confidentiality, simultaneously seeks to establish a program culture of openness. While this may seem contradictory in theory, it is simpler in practice. It is not difficult to distinguish confidential content from work with parents and group psychotherapy from the general daily flow of the program classroom. The therapeutic inclusion program classroom/milieu encourages an open-door atmosphere and full integration into the school. Within the relationship-based culture of the program classroom, the staff cultivates an atmosphere where talking about one's emotional state, life at home, struggles, and successes is both normal and safe. The classroom is an open therapeutic milieu where the student is invited to experience themselves within safe relationships with therapeutic educators who are working closely with their parent. This leads to a sense of containment and cohesiveness which can facilitate movement toward emotional maturity.

Students with significant social/emotional/behavioral challenges have often been ostracized in the school environment. They have received the message that their feelings and behaviors are "too much." Many students arrive to the therapeutic inclusion program making little or no distinction between their emotional state and their behavior. Some students have bundled their feelings and behaviors together in an internal compartment labeled "rejected." They may arrive at the troubling conclusion that some of their feelings and problems are unspeakable.

In the therapeutic milieu, alongside behavioral interventions to ensure a safe environment for all, students receive the message that their feelings and their safe expression are very welcome. To counter the feeling that their issues are unspeakable, the therapeutic milieu seeks to create an environment where a broad range of topics can be safely talked about. Educators encourage conversation about experiences outside school, home life, cultural traditions, religious practice, and more. The educators model that it is safe and rewarding to be curious about others, and to bring your whole experience and self into the conversation. This encourages the developing sense that the problems students are struggling with can also be safely talked about. The open and copious communication home helps the parent feel secure about their child's work and progress in the therapeutic inclusion program.

In the event where the home environment and relationships are not sufficiently safe, then the therapeutic work is much more difficult, and a more complicated approach must be carefully negotiated in collaboration with the program supervisor.

The exception to the open flow of communication from school to home about events and conversations in the therapeutic inclusion program is meeting, or group psychotherapy. Group psychotherapy maintains basic therapeutic confidentiality best practices in a student therapy group. Apart from issues that present an immediate safety threat, topics brought up in group psychotherapy can remain in session. This helps provide an environment where students may feel safe enough to talk about issues they find particularly difficult.

The mechanics of home and school communication in the therapeutic inclusion program

The method and style of parent communication used by the therapeutic inclusion program was developed at Community Therapeutic Day School in Lexington, Massachusetts. It is also described, as well as further explicated, in Daniel Reinstein's book *To Hold and Be Held* (2006).

Communication between home and school within the therapeutic inclusion program consists of two primary elements. One is a home–school communication journal, which contains daily narrative style communications between home and school. The second is 30-minute weekly parent phone calls.

Program co-leaders share the task of leading parent communication in order to build personalized relationships. Generally, the program co-leaders would take on equal amounts, or as close as possible given the number of students in the program. These parent relationships are part of the therapeutic support for the student, and the co-leaders will receive support for the parent work as part of supervision.

The communication book

The communication book is a blank journal, often a classic composition notebook, which is used as a written communication vehicle between home and school. The communication book travels between home and school with the student. The program co-leader working with the student's parent is responsible for writing a note home by the end of each school day. Typically, these notes can range in length from a short paragraph to a couple of pages. An example can be found in Appendix B.

In the event that there are literacy and/or language barriers to this communication method, accommodations should be made so that the parent can receive the communication.

The purpose of the communication book is to build and maintain the home–school connection. Daily communication strengthens the school–home relationship. While a daily phone call would be valuable, it is impractical logistically. The communication book methodology allows staff to update the books during the school day. The books also create a helpful record of events that can be useful when considering trends and patterns.

Interpreting the written word is much different than having a conversation. Therefore, the notes to home should be a narrative reporting of the facts of the day. This can be done in a warm and personable way, while sticking to the factual and observable. More sensitive and nuanced material should be reserved for phone conversations or other live, two-way communication.

The information in the communication book assists the parent in connecting with their child and supporting the work at home. The parent has a sense for their child's school day, and with this information is better able to engage with their child. While important and timely information is often communicated in the communication book, the relatively mundane day-to-day details that are passed on are just as therapeutic for their cumulative effect. Representative details such as what was played at recess, an encouraging comment from a teacher, and academic work updates are also important to include. When the student hears about regular school day details from their parent, the student feels seen and held between home and school.

Our student's significant social, emotional, and behavioral needs often demand intense staff and parent attention. We suggest remaining mindful that academic learning is a central purpose of school, and ensuring that every daily note contains some academic information.

Parents are also asked to write a daily note about events at home, so that the student experiences the home–school connection with their therapeutic teachers as well. Notes from home provide timely and useful information, which informs the work in the milieu and the school. The therapeutic program staff reads and passes the books among themselves every school morning.

Parents vary in their engagement with the communication book and communication in general. Some parents read and write in the book every single school day. Other parents read the book daily, but tend not to write in it. And yet other parents tend not to read or write in the communication book. As therapeutic educators, it is important that the nonjudgmental approach extends through the mechanics of parent communication. In practice, this means that every parent receives a daily note home, regardless of how they engage with the communication book. Similarly, program co-leaders must persist at offering and being available for weekly parent phone calls, even when parents are not making use of it. It is the program's role to be a dependable partner, whether or not the parent are also able to be reliable in their communication.

The parent, regardless of their level of participation in parent communication, should always experience the message that their full participation is welcome, and that they are treated with the same respect and care regardless of their ability to engage with communication.

While the communication book is part of the confidential therapeutic work of the program, it should be kept in mind that as a physical object traveling with the student, it can be lost and picked up by someone else. Any material that may feel particularly private to the child or family should be saved for the weekly conversation, or an extra phone call if necessary.

Weekly parent conversations

Weekly parent conversations usually take the form of phone calls. They can also occur in person at the school, or over a secure video conferencing platform. The parent conversation is with the designated program co-leader who is responsible for ensuring that their communication book is updated every day.

The child's legal parent(s) should be invited to participate in the weekly conversations. Children have a wide range of family compositions. In a situation where there is more than one parent involved with a student, that creates a parent team. When working with parent teams, there are a number of possible logistical arrangements, including conference calls or alternating calls.

Most often in a parent team, one parent will take on the role of point-person for school communication.

The parent communication is part of the therapeutic care of the student. The parent is not the subject of the therapeutic work. Instead, they are usually the central part of their child's care team. The parent represents their child to the program as the adults who know their child best, and they are the legal holder's of their child's confidentiality.

While the communication book should be used for fact-based reporting, the weekly parent conversation provides a venue for more nuanced conversation. Different parents make different uses of the weekly conversation. Parents and staff can collaborate on designing effective interventions that have buy-in and understanding at both home and school. Many parents appreciate being part of the process of developing interventions that take place in school and make crucial creative contributions. Some parents use the opportunity to get input and collaboration regarding responses and interventions at home, combining their expertise about their child with the staff members expertise as a therapeutic educator. The therapeutic educator's empathetic and knowledgeable ear is sometimes the most helpful element of the weekly conversation, especially given that the therapeutic educator is also engaged in a care relationship with the student.

Email

In the therapeutic inclusion program, outgoing email should only be used for scheduling and other logistical communication. Emails are not secure methods for confidential, therapeutic information. School email systems are especially insecure because they are often accessible by district tech experts and administrators. The communication book provides a daily opportunity for communication. If extra communication is needed, program staff can make a call to home.

Parents should be apprised of the lack of security on email systems, though they are free to send emails with whatever information they wish. Program staff can respond to therapeutic content in the communication book or on the phone.

Special events and parent group

There should be at least a couple of opportunities for program families to gather in the therapeutic classroom over the course of the school year. The COVID-19 pandemic forced programs to have these gatherings virtually. Though gathering in person is a better experience, the virtual gathering was still very positive for the program community. In a public school setting, administrators unfamiliar with the therapeutic inclusion model may be wary of bringing together a group of parents of students in a special education program for confidentiality reasons. The program supervisor can be a helpful resource in explaining the necessity of the familial group and gathering to hesitant administrators.

A back to school event in October falls at a good time of year. The program has had enough time to establish routines, while it is still early enough in the academic year to maximize the benefits of connecting the student's families to the classroom. Students enjoy showing their families the classroom, their desks, the places they learn, and the places they play. Having occupied the space, parents can feel more connected to the events and stories of the classroom. Special events also provide an opportunity for families to connect and support one other.

Additionally, a regular parent support group provides an excellent opportunity for parents to connect with one another, while also providing a forum for parent ideas and concerns to be addressed directly. Parent group should be run by the program co-leaders and can occur weekly, bi-weekly, or monthly. The varying schedules and needs of parents can present scheduling challenges, as well as the scheduling limitations of the program co-leaders. Parent group may not be a practical possibility for every therapeutic inclusion program; however, it is a helpful element to keep in mind and implement if conditions allow.

Collateral contacts

Dependent upon parental consent, program co-leaders will develop relationships with outside professionals who are working with their students. Connecting with other helpers and their perspectives aids in understanding the whole child, and in being part of an integrated care team. Parents have discretion on whether to sign off on these connections. Given their approval, appropriate release-of-information forms must be signed and filed.

Curiosity is the leading guide in forming relationships with outside professionals, who may have the opportunity to see a side of the students not seen at school, or bring an expert lens that is illuminating. Outside professionals can include therapists, psychiatrists, recreational programs, summer programs, private music teachers, and more. School-based reporting is often useful for psychiatrists in making medication determinations. Program staff should seek to remain aware of medication changes and to keep a record of them in a secure place at school. School staff are well positioned to provide observational feedback as changes are made.

The repair journal

Henry's mother and the program counselor built a collaborative relationship through the communication book and weekly phone calls over time. This relationship was strong enough to hold together even as inevitable distress tested the system, most notably as Henry contemplated personal change.

As happens for Henry in this story, a spike in a behavior can occur before the behavior changes. This is a stage where the student continues to feel attached to the behavior, while simultaneously experiencing that the behavior is no longer sufficiently rewarding, given the therapeutic intervention within the program. This circumstance does not feel tolerable. Something will have to change. Will it be the behavior, or the intervention? The therapeutic inclusion program must consider these questions as well, and the answers are not foregone conclusions.

Henry began in the therapeutic inclusion program as he entered second grade at the end of August. He was a bright and intellectually curious young person, who valued friendship and wanted social success. Henry carried diagnoses of ADHD and generalized anxiety disorder. These diagnoses matched his presentation. But, like most people, he was better understood in descriptive terms than diagnostic.

Henry was smart, sensitive, and had a clever sense of humor. His chief difficulty was extraordinary impulsivity. The program counselor, Mr. Twomey, imagined Henry's "wiring" as all copper, with hardly a semiconductor to be found. Henry was not only extraordinarily impulsive, he was also extraordinarily sensitive. These two qualities combined in a way that heightened the challenges of his behavior. He was quick to perceive a threat and took defensive action in a flash.

Given his sensitive threat perception, Henry could experience a threat in someone else winning a game, in being passed over with his hand up in class, in someone else having a desired object, or in the lack of control over his environment and activities typical of being a student. When a threat was perceived, Henry would take defensive action. His reaction could only be seen as defensive by looking through the lens of his threat perspective. To those around him, his defenses were offensive. He would lash out verbally, and sometimes physically, at peers at a rate of about one or two incidences over the course of two weeks. The quality of his physical attacks was much less forceful than he was capable of. Henry seemed to perform aggression more than behave dangerously. However, he was crossing into peer's personal space threateningly, which was a significant concern.

Henry steadfastly did not want to apologize to any of his peers for these transgressions. Mr. Twomey made some effort to support him in apologizing. Henry's unwillingness was interpreted by Mr. Twomey as an inability to afford the ego expenditure he perceived. The program was responsible for maintaining a safe classroom atmosphere and protecting Henry from the social stigmatization of further boundary crossing. With Henry unable to express remorse along with an intention to stay safe, the program determined that Henry would need to be closely monitored at all times, including lunch and recess. This was done while attempting to minimize the stigma of this intervention to the extent possible.

A parent and staff collaboration

While providing Henry with the intervention of constant staff support, the intervention of the repair journal was developed through a creative mutual collaboration between his parents and teachers. The collaboration strengthened the working relationship, and the relationship welcomed collaboration. These two therapeutic factors are mutually reinforcing.

Henry's parents were married, and his mother Alisha largely managed the communication with school and the therapeutic inclusion program. She and Mr. Twomey used the communication book daily to report back and forth about home and school and used the 30-minute phone calls with Mr. Twomey each week to collaborate on behalf of Henry.

Alisha and Mr. Twomey shared concern over Henry's lashing out, both for its impact on others and its social effect on himself. Alisha wanted Henry to experience that every day was a new opportunity to have a safe, fun, and excellent day. Mr. Twomey endorsed this, but also prioritized supporting Henry in developing an age-appropriate understanding of the interconnectedness of events over time. For instance, being closely supervised all day was annoying for Henry. It also represented a point in a longer narrative which included him not being reliably safe with peers. Henry certainly had the cognitive strength to understand this narrative, and that his previous incidences of lashing out carried meaning in his current moment. But, Henry very much wished that this was not the case. He wished that previous episodes of lashing out were without meaning, and that the all day, close supervision could also be wished away. This wishing, and lack of appreciation for the interconnectedness of events, did nothing to slow him down when he again perceived a threat.

The communication book helped connect the daily events of home and school, in order to help Henry experience the cohesive home and school connection and collaboration. During their phone calls, Alisha and Mr. Twomey discussed how to support Henry in both environments. They discussed how to combine the fresh opportunity of a new day, with an age-appropriate understanding of the cumulative effect of events over time.

It was clear that Henry was not ready to do repair with the peers he had lashed out toward. In early October, in order to preserve a path toward a decrease in close supervision that could feel safe for Henry and his peers, Mr. Twomey started maintaining a "repair journal" in a yellow notebook. It was modeled in the style of a home repair list. It noted which relationships needed repair, why they needed repair (briefly what had happened), and a box to check off when the repair was complete. Instead of engaging in a direct student and staff struggle around apologizing, the repair list was simply an object in a cabinet. In order to have safe and fun relationships that did not require close supervision, Henry had some repair to do.

This attached the apologies to their real meaning, instead of what develops when school staff is in the position of convincing students to apologize. As many parents and teachers have experienced, an apology insisted upon by an authority (i.e., teacher or parent) takes on meaning within the child's relationship with the authority and tends to distract from the injury and peer relationship that actually calls for repair.

While the repair journal helped to reduce the sense of student and staff interpersonal struggle around the issue of apologies, they remained an exquisitely sensitive matter for Henry. Perhaps on a deep level, it represented a call for change in his orientation toward personal responsibility, as well as in his defensive response of lashing out at others.

Upon returning from winter break to school in January, Henry was very angry about the persistent existence of the repair journal. It had not disappeared. At Mr. Twomey's mention of the repair journal in the apparently calm aftermath of an incident with a classmate, Henry lashed out at him physically. Amidst this, Alisha and Mr. Twomey continued their communication and collaboration. Was it time for a "new day"? Henry argued to Mr. Twomey and Alisha that his classmates had probably forgotten about some of these incidents at this point. This was likely correct, Mr. Twomey agreed. However, while Mr. Twomey felt he had a responsibility to be helpful to all students at the school, he had a special responsibility to Henry. Helping him hold on to the meaning of events, and the narrative within his relationships at school was something Mr. Twomey was doing chiefly to support him. Mr. Twomey talked about this with Henry and with Alisha.

Alisha was concerned about Henry's rising anger about the repair journal, and wondered if there was a way to "put it on the back burner." While Mr. Twomey had a sense that they were operating in a meaningful space for Henry, he too was concerned about Henry's level of frustration. The repair journal was "back burner" by nature. How could it continue to hold meaning if it were to do less than sit in the cabinet, added to when necessary?

Alisha was able to tolerate Henry's mounting frustration, but noted the lack of concrete reward and positivity. To compensate she felt that Henry could use a gentle incentive to sweeten the benefits of making repairs. The family acquired a LEGO® set, which the program staff divided into sequential Zip Lock® bags. He could bring one home with each repair. This reward was fitting as it represented parts that built (integrated) toward a whole, mirroring the sense of integration and meaning of the repairs themselves.

Alisha also suggested that Mr. Twomey and Henry could start a second "repaired journal," which Mr. Twomey instantly recognized as a great idea. Mr. Twomey acquired a dramatically and heroically decorated Star Wars® notebook, in which they would record only entries of successful repair. In this month of January Henry began to experiment with some repairs, earning the sequential LEGO® bags to bring home, while Mr. Twomey and Henry recorded his successes in the repaired journal together.

This did not bring about an immediate change in his pattern of behavior, which in fact intensified before it improved. But, significant change did follow relatively quickly. As the repair journal records, Henry's last incident of lashing out verbally or physically at a peer during their two school years together came about five months into their work in the therapeutic inclusion program together, on February 3.

A few weeks later, on an otherwise pedestrian Tuesday, February 25, Henry came to school ready to complete his repair journal. Henry wrote a series of complete repairs, or apology notes. Each was addressed by name to the recipient and signed by Henry. Each included an apology, and what he was apologizing for. As Henry worked through this, he received momentum-building goodwill and positive attention from the school community. He was able to reflect on how it was feeling, and he said it felt really good. Inwardly, Mr. Twomey perceived that Henry's vulnerable fear that apologizing would be an experience of personal diminishment was not bearing out. Alisha reported that Henry carried this ability to repair and apologize forward, and it stayed with him.

The collaboration between home and school created environmental circumstances where it was possible for Henry to develop stronger self-regulation, understand the interconnectedness of events in an age-appropriate manner, and become a steward of his relationships. Mr. Twomey brought his creativity and therapeutic understanding to the collaboration. Alisha brought her own creativity (along with support and consultation with her spouse), as well as her deeply understood sense for the limits of Henry's frustration tolerance and his need for more positive framing and reinforcement. From within this careful attention and cooperation between home and school, Henry felt safe enough to allow for vulnerability and to try new ways of relating to his peers. It is fair to surmise that the intervention would not have weathered the storm of Henry's frustration without the trust built within the teacher–parent relationship. It is also safe to surmise that the intervention would not have been successful without Alisha's understanding of her child, and her positive and creative contributions.

Conclusion

Work with parents is a key element of the therapeutic inclusion program. As a therapeutic component functioning for the benefit of the student, parent work is part of the program's clinically supervised therapies. Most of the communication occurs through the daily communication book and weekly conversation. As an element of the student's therapies, these communications are confidential.

While relatively surface-level interventions are effective for many students, children generally arrive in the therapeutic inclusion program because previous interventions have not been sufficiently effective. An appreciation of the environment and its impact on unconscious motivations is part of the therapeutic inclusion program. Resistance to change, and transference and countertransference are also recognized as playing important roles. The program co-leaders manage parent communication, with consultation from the program supervisor. These psychological concepts can become part of the parent conversation, usually using plain language. Most important in the teacher-parent relationship is the program co-leader's empathetic ear, their respect for the deep knowledge and experience the parent brings, and their invitation to collaboration on behalf of the student.

With these elements in place, the working relationship between the therapeutic inclusion program and the student's parent is an integral part of the therapeutic work. The two environments of home and school retain their unique character, while building collaboration and connection in a way that is experienced by the student. This is a home–school environment that can weather distress and facilitate the child's movement toward maturity and health.

References

Freud, S., & Breuer, J. (1895/1955) *Studies on hysteria. In Strachey, J. (Ed. & Trans.), The standard edition of the complete psychological works of Sigmund Freud. Vol. 2*. Hogarth.

Gray, C. (2015). *The new social story book*. Future Horizons.

Hartzell, M., & Siegel, D. J. (2014). *Parenting from the inside out: How a deeper self-understanding can help you raise children who thrive*. Jeremy P. Tarcher/Penguin.

Reinstein, D. K. (2006). *To hold and be held: The therapeutic school as a holding environment*. Routledge.

Winnicott, D. W. (1965). *The maturational processes and the facilitating environment: Studies in the theory of emotional development*. International Universities Press.

9 A Resilient Structure Part One

The Truss and the Program Staff

The core structure of the therapeutic inclusion program is introduced in this chapter, using the metaphor of the weight-bearing truss as a resilient structure. A truss has three sides that mutually support each other. This chapter describes the dedicated program staff as one side of the truss. Subsequent chapters will cover the supervision and administrative sides of the structure. A narrative demonstrating how the dedicated staff of the program can work cooperatively to overcome inevitable interpersonal challenges rounds out the chapter.

A resilient structure

The therapeutic inclusion program is designed for students with significant social, emotional, and behavioral difficulties. The work of serving this population of students is in great part the work of accepting, holding, and processing the distress they are experiencing. In most cases, the students and families have largely been alone with the distress emanating from mental health issues, neurological issues, and traumas. While they might have relationships with some doctors, therapists, and specialists, they are unlikely to have had a partner in compassionate day-after-day care like they experience in the therapeutic inclusion program.

There is a lived and experienced message of the program to the child and their parents in relationship to the distress they are experiencing. It is "we will help hold this with you." Working together to help hold the student's and parent's distress is perhaps the most challenging, effective, and satisfying part of the work.

In order for the therapeutic inclusion program to hold this weight, it must be well supported. Borrowing a weight-bearing concept from engineering, envision a truss. A truss is a triangular structure that can support significant weight because it disperses tension among its three beams. The therapeutic inclusion program is also supported by a structure made of three beams, which disperses the weight of the distress the program encounters (see Figure 9.1).

The three beams that support the work of the therapeutic inclusion program are (1) the program staff, (2) supervision, and (3) administration.

The roles of the program supervisor and the administrative role are described in detail in Chapters Ten and Eleven.

DOI: 10.4324/9781003270478-10

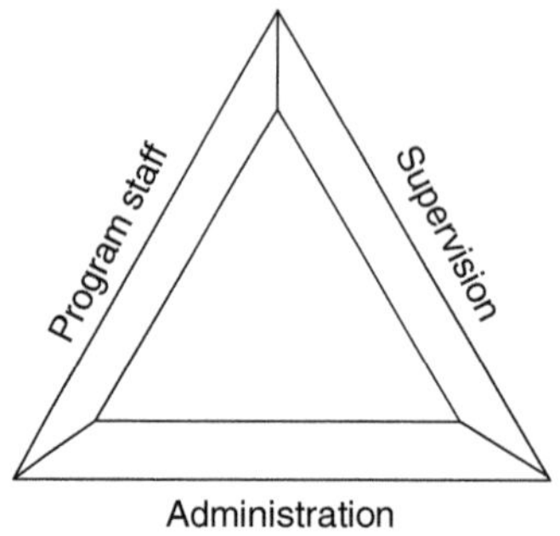

Figure 9.1 A truss. Image by Benjamin Murray.

The therapeutic program staff have the most demanding, emotionally intensive, and work-intensive role in the triangle. The program staff represents the side of the truss that will initially encounter the weight of distress. The therapeutic program staff provides direct therapeutic and educational service to the students, coordinates with other school staff and outside professionals, and works with the student's parents. Significantly, the program staff also represent the part of the triangle for whom the therapeutic inclusion program is their full-time job.

The roles of the program supervisor and administrators are in support and guidance of the program staff's direct work. Administrators are likely to have some interaction with students and their parents. The program supervisor is most likely to have very little direct interaction with students and their families.

The therapeutic inclusion program is anchored by two program staff members. This leadership team is comprised of a special education teacher and a mental health counselor. The rest of the dedicated program staff would be paraprofessionals in most cases.

In the therapeutic inclusion program model, the counselor serves as the therapeutic leader, and the special education teacher as the educational leader. However, these divisions of expertise and labor are flexible. Over time in a well-functioning program, the special education teacher will become an increasingly skilled therapeutic practitioner, and the counselor will develop growing skills as an educator. In consultation with administration and therapeutic supervision, the program co-leaders are the center of decision-making and operation of the therapeutic inclusion program.

For the purposes of an initial description, we will imagine a single therapeutic inclusion program room, bridging three grades, with seven students. Spread across three grades, the program would likely require two paraprofessionals. This staffing is necessary because most students in the program will require a therapeutic inclusion program staffer in their general education classes. There also has to be some flexibility for lunches, prep times, breaks, and inevitable scheduling complications.

Dedicated program staff

Special education teacher

The special education teacher should be appropriately certified for the grade levels being served, as a teacher of students with moderate or severe disabilities. Though there will likely not be any additional certifications or formal trainings required for this position, the special education teacher must be interested in and dedicated to therapeutic teaching. A special educator who has training and experience teaching students with moderate to significant behaviors, including de-escalation and restraint, and enjoys working with this population of students, would be a good fit. An orientation toward collaboration, curiosity, and creativity is crucial.

Counselor

The counselor should be trained in mental health counseling, social work, or school counseling. They should have an orientation toward relationship-based work and therapeutic work in groups. Teamed with a high-quality supervisor, these qualifications may be enough for a counselor gifted with curiosity who is excited about learning. The therapeutic supervision model which facilitates counselor development is described in Chapter Ten.

Ultimately, between the program counselor and their supervisor, there must reside a sophisticated understanding of the recapitulation of family dynamics within the group, transference and countertransference, resistance, process-oriented group psychotherapy, and parent support.

The counselor's supervisor should be an individual with more relevant experience in these therapeutic realms than the program counselor. In the event where the program counselor is highly experienced, their supervisor should have at least an equal amount of experience.

Administrators should cast a wider job-candidate net than they are accustomed to in order to find the right person for the role of program counselor, as well as an individual to supervise the program counselor. Most university school counseling programs are preparing counselors for therapeutic work built around responsive strategies (tools in the toolbox), behavior intervention plans, and supporting trauma-informed schools. These areas of focus are of tremendous value in schools. However, they do not necessarily prepare a school counselor to lead a therapeutic milieu, lead process-oriented group psychotherapy, and work within the supervisory relationship that is de rigueur in most mental health work. Because of this, administrators should consider candidates within a range of mental health counseling degrees and backgrounds, who are interested in working with children and adolescents, along with school counselors.

Paraprofessionals

Paraprofessionals are likely to complete the therapeutic inclusion program staff. Similarly to the program leadership, the key qualities in program paraprofessionals are curiosity, creativity, and interest in collaboration. The program leadership is ultimately responsible for designing and supervising therapeutic and educational interventions. That being said, the therapeutic inclusion program thrives on collaboration. Through time in the classrooms together and regular meetings, all members of the staff are expected to contribute collaboratively.

As described in Chapter Ten, the paraprofessionals will be supervised therapeutically and educationally by the program co-leadership, and in some cases the program therapeutic supervisor. These regular meetings are always oriented toward the opportunity for staff members to grow in their understanding, abilities, and creativity.

Paraprofessionals must be prepared and able to deliver academic instruction and therapeutic interventions. They must have the patience and temperament conducive toward working with students with significant social, emotional, and behavioral difficulties.

Collaboration and communication in the therapeutic inclusion program

The program co-leaders and the paraprofessionals are the dedicated staff of the therapeutic inclusion program. From this core, communication and collaboration branches outward in several directions including (1) parents of students in the program, (2) general education teachers, (3) specialists(such as speech and language pathologists and occupational therapists), (4) program supervisor, (5) BCBAs, and (6) administrators.

This section offers a model for the frequencies and durations of the regular meetings that support collaboration between the program, the rest of the school, and parents. Included are specific frequencies and durations. These are presented for clarity, but are not rigid. The needs of each school and program will lead to variation.

The key part of the meeting structure is regular, dependable, and collaborative communication. This must be structured into the functioning of the program in order to be effective and sustainable. The model of regular meetings mirrors the supervision model from therapeutic work in mental health (described in Chapter Ten), and in this manner supports the various parts of the collaborative system that is the therapeutic inclusion program.

The program co-leaders manage most of this communication. The aim is for parents, specialists, teachers, and administrators, to have positive, collaborative, and supportive experiences when working with the program. In this way, working in collaboration with the therapeutic inclusion program can be experienced as helpful and rewarding, rather than simply another responsibility. In fact, the collaborative support offered by the therapeutic inclusion program improves classroom experiences for general education teachers, specialists, and administrators, leading them to want to collaborate with the program year after year.

These working relationships are maintained through regularly scheduled meetings. The recurring and predictable time and duration of the meeting greatly diminishes the stress that can arise around such questions as What is worth communicating? When is the right time to communicate? Teachers and specialists look forward to these meetings because they know they will be listened to carefully, and worked with collaboratively. Within these meetings and relationships the program co-leaders model core therapeutic values of careful empathic listening and positive regard.

General education teachers

The therapeutic inclusion program students should be grouped within one general education classroom per grade, otherwise managing class support and meetings becomes greatly complicated and resource heavy. Collaborating general education teachers will benefit from a 30-minute weekly meeting with the program co-leaders.

The orientation of the program co-leaders in meeting with the general education teacher is to support the classroom teacher in their role of educating the students in the program. It is important for the program co-leaders to respect this responsibility held by the general education teachers, and to focus on how to best collaborate with and assist them in this task. Support from the therapeutic inclusion program lifts the experience of the general education teacher and their classroom in a way that creates a richer and more rewarding experience for all. This is achieved with the understanding that there is one leader in a general education classroom, the general education classroom teacher. The therapeutic inclusion program staff should seek to aid that teacher in fulfilling their vision for the classroom, while helping it meet the needs of the therapeutic inclusion program students.

Administrators

The program co-leaders meet with a member or members of the administrative chain, such as the principal, assistant principal, or special education coordinator weekly for 30 minutes. It is also important for the program's therapeutic supervisor to remain engaged with administration. This could occur separately, or during the same weekly meeting.

Administrators can help navigate issues that can arise when the needs of a therapeutic inclusion program are different from the traditional needs of a public school. Most frequently, these are circumstances where established school policy, likely designed before the establishment of a therapeutic inclusion program, is not a fit for a therapeutic inclusion program. For example, the school may have behavior and discipline policies that do not match the individualized approaches required in the program.

It is also important for the program co-leaders to keep the administration apprised of developments within the program. The program is creative by nature, and administrators must be informed so that they can influence the creativity, give direction when needed, and avoid being caught off guard about program developments.

Specialists

As dedicated special education professionals, specialists such as speech and language pathologists and occupational therapists are usually well-prepared to understand and collaborate with the therapeutic inclusion program. A monthly 30-minute meeting between the program co-leaders and the team of specialists works well.

Parents

An approach to parent communication is covered in detail in Chapter Eight. In terms of frequency and duration, the communication consists of weekly 30-minute phone calls with one of the program co-leaders, as well as the daily communication journal sent between home and school.

A monthly parent group can also be of great benefit. The group facilitates support among the parents and is able to bring issues and distress relevant to the program that may arise outside of the school day back into the program so that they can be addressed. The monthly parent group is led by the program co-leaders.

Board certified behavior analysts

BCBAs are expected personnel in the public education landscape. BCBAs stem from the behaviorist wing of psychology. Behaviorism is appealing to school administrators for a number of reasons. Its systematized nature lends itself to methods and research which can be relatively easily understood by lay people. BCBAs have a range of research-based interventions that are helpful to many students.

The therapeutic inclusion program's orientation toward behaviorism is that behaviorist interventions are an indispensable tool in the effort to support students with significant behavioral difficulties. The therapeutic inclusion program is a relationship-based approach. This means the relationship comes first. Once safe and supportive relationships are established, behaviorist interventions such as behavior intervention plans can be introduced within those relationships. There is no timeline for this, as it is dependent on the unique presentation and development of each student. Often, it is quickly appropriate and helpful to introduce behavior intervention plans. Sometimes, it is never helpful or appropriate for a given student.

It is helpful for the program co-leaders to have a weekly 30-minute consult with a BCBA. The BCBA can consult about behavioral interventions, suggest improvements, and help informatively and creatively when designing behavior intervention plans.

Adults as social models for students

Children are sensitive to the culture and emotional content of the relationships among the adults that care for them. The program staff, in all of its interactions pertaining to the program, are modeling for the students how to communicate and be part of a group. The structure, reliability, and style of staff communication directly impact the students.

When the program and school staff are working smoothly, the benefits to the program are obvious. There is a sense of ease, spontaneity, and shared understanding. However, disagreement and frustration are inevitable parts of collaborative group work. In the therapeutic inclusion program, disagreement and frustration among adults represent another kind of therapeutic opportunity. It is an opportunity for the staff to model for the students how a group works through differences.

This often occurs in adult meetings, away from the students. However, differences can be worked out among adults in the classroom with the students present, depending on the circumstances and the working relationships. Whether students witness the staff communication as they work through the issue or not, the students benefit from the process.

Program students sense the staff experiencing interpersonal difficulty and witness the staff sticking together and working through it. For many students with social, emotional, and behavioral difficulties their intense sensitivity leads them to fear that interpersonal rifts inevitably lead to loss. The staff's ongoing work for the program shows that interpersonal rifts occur in all groups, and that with communication and thoughtful attention they can be repaired. This is deeply reassuring.

Communication among adults furthering the therapeutic process

Mr. Hurley was a paraprofessional in the therapeutic inclusion program who supported two second-grade members of the program in their general education classroom, as well as in the therapeutic milieu. The therapeutic inclusion program was co-led by counselor, Ms. Ruiz, and special education teacher, Ms. Davis.

Ms. Thomson was the second-grade teacher leading the general education classroom, in her first year working with the program. Ms. Thomson was tentative to work with students from the therapeutic inclusion program. Before the development of the therapeutic inclusion program within her school, she, like almost all general education teachers, had students in her class with challenging behavior and a lack of support or tools to be able to support them within the confines of her classroom. Ms. Thomson wanted to be excited about working with the therapeutic inclusion program as an opportunity to support a more diverse and inclusive class, though she did not have a thorough understanding of how this would be different than her previous experiences. Ms. Thomson did not have the comfort to share this with the program co-leaders at the beginning of their work together, yet later opened up about her initial fear and subsequent positive experience as the relationship progressed.

Ms. Thomson was also anxious as she had experienced other situations within the school where collaboration with other adults had proven difficult. Additional adult support in the classroom is highly valuable. However, another set of adult ideas, and potential judgments, can be anxiety provoking. Her previous experience suggested that it may be better to go it alone, rather than manage the issues that can arise with another adult in the room.

The program paraprofessional, Mr. Hurley, was skilled, talented, and socially reserved among the staff. The therapeutic inclusion program students presented with a high level of need as they adjusted to second grade in Ms. Thomson's classroom. Mr. Hurley was busy carefully responding to their presentation according to plans that had been designed in the therapeutic inclusion program with input from Ms. Thomson.

In keeping with the program model, the program co-leaders Ms. Ruiz and Ms. Davis met weekly with Ms. Thomson. The program co-leaders listened and supported Ms. Thomson as she adjusted to including a wider range of social, emotional, and behavioral presentations in the classroom. The program co-leaders also met weekly with Mr. Hurley during the program staff meeting.

One of the second graders from the program had a tendency to loudly verbalize distress. The other student from the program would sometimes take refuge under his desk when agitated. Ms. Davis, Ms. Ruiz, and Ms. Thomson discussed under what circumstances it was appropriate for either student to leave the classroom, and where there were opportunities to broaden the work possible within an inclusive classroom. These are difficult and subjective decisions, best navigated by listening carefully and respecting viewpoints.

The program co-leaders, as well as Ms. Thomson and Mr. Hurley, felt that meeting together to discuss this could be helpful. However, Mr. Hurley's limited paraprofessional schedule did not allow for it. Ms. Davis and Ms. Ruiz did some work acting as a communication conduit between Ms. Thomson and Mr. Hurley, as they developed guidelines of when to stay in the classroom and when to take a break. This was convenient since the program co-leaders met with both educators. Notwithstanding, the program co-leaders were wary of establishing a central pattern of carrying communication between Ms. Thomson and Mr. Hurley.

After a few weeks, Ms. Thomson shared with the co-leaders that it made her uneasy at moments when she was leading the whole class, and Mr. Hurley was responding to in-the-moment developments. She understood that Mr. Hurley was being quiet in his interventions in order to minimize disruption to the class, but it was sometimes difficult for Ms. Thomson to have another adult active in a crucial role in the classroom, and to not know for certain what was transpiring.

Mr. Hurley and and Ms. Thomson did not tend to communicate directly very much. Ms. Thomson's demanding work of managing a large group and Mr. Hurley's socially reserved nature combined to activate Ms. Thomson's anxieties about having other adults working in her classroom. Her opportunity for direct communication with Mr. Hurley being limited, Ms. Thomson's previous negative experience with judgmental colleagues started to fill the unknown space.

The program co-leaders, Ms. Ruiz and Ms. Davis, continued their weekly meetings with Ms. Thomson, and with the program staff. The co-leaders heard what was developing from both perspectives. Seeing both colleagues from a foundation of positive regard, they saw the opportunity to strengthen communication and working relationships with the program. This would be to the benefit of everyone involved, most importantly the students.

Ms. Thomson and Mr. Hurley needed more communication. Ms. Ruiz and Ms. Diaz resolved to use the program structure to support their colleagues in strengthening their working relationship. During their meetings with Ms. Thomson, the program co-leaders reassured her that Mr. Hurley is open and available to check in about events in the classroom. During their meetings with Mr. Hurley, they checked in with him so that he could anticipate that Ms. Thomson intended to talk to him about how things are going in the classroom.

With this gentle nudge and reassurance from program co-leaders, the two educators were able to establish better communication. Ms. Thomson felt more comfortable, and Mr. Hurley appreciated the increased communication. The improved communication and decrease in stress improved their work with the program students and the classroom.

While the positive improvements were significant, the pitfalls that were avoided are equally significant. Despite the presence of two dedicated and kind educators, the ingredients were present for growing mistrust and a difficult working relationship. The resulting stress and miscommunications would certainly be stressful for the educators and would negatively impact the students. Ms. Ruiz and Ms. Davis, in their role as the hub of program communication, were able to help convert a fraught disconnect into a growth opportunity that benefitted staff and students.

Conclusion

Complex interpersonal circumstances like those between Ms. Thomson and Mr. Hurley play out in myriad permutations over the course of an academic year. With a predictable structure in place, organized around regular collaborative meetings, the educators in and working with the program do great collaborative work. Just as valuable, they use the structure to work through the inevitable difficulties that come up in the course of collaboration.

In this way the staff practices and models the same principles in their working relationships that imbues their work with students. In instances both in class and behind the scenes, the students experience a group of adults working together through thoughtful communication, as well as working through difficulties. The staff is always modeling for the students how to be a member of a group.

Therapeutic inclusion program core philosophies of positive regard, respectful collaboration, and providing room for autonomy and growth are present in all the activities of the program. This includes direct services with the student and runs through meetings with parents, colleagues, and administrators.

Regular meetings facilitate the reliable and effective functioning of the therapeutic inclusion program. A program co-leader can expect to spend about three hours per week in scheduled meetings collaborating with colleagues, and another one or two hours per week meeting with parents over phone, videoconference, or in person.

10 A Resilient Structure Part Two

The Therapeutic Supervision Model

This chapter explains why a supervision model is required for the therapeutic inclusion program. Supervision is the second beam of the truss that mutually supports the program. The structure of supervision within the therapeutic inclusion program model is somewhat flexible, mostly dependent on the experience and expertise of the program co-leaders. Two supervision models are shared in this chapter, one with experienced program co-leaders, and another with less experienced program co-leaders. A narrative from our work in the field illustrates thoughtful and creative supervision, in parallel process with the care taking place throughout the program.

Supervision required

As described in Chapter Seven, an important function of the therapeutic inclusion program is helping to hold the distress experienced by students and their families. The professional support and collaboration facilitated through the supervision model is necessary for this work.

The therapeutic inclusion program uses a therapeutic supervision model. To most mental health professionals, this would be an obvious assumption. However, supervision in many school districts and programs has been dismissed as unnecessary. From a therapeutic standpoint, this is unjustifiable. From a school administrative standpoint this develops due to budget concerns, lack of understanding of therapeutic work, and fear of complex therapeutic work.

Supervision is required for quality therapeutic work and for the maintenance of a functioning therapeutic inclusion program. The therapeutic supervision model provides direct therapeutic service providers (the therapeutic inclusion program staff) with sophisticated support. The staff requires this support in order to encounter, hold, and process significant emotional distress. Most private therapeutic schools use a therapeutic supervision model in order to responsibly and effectively work with complicated and emotionally challenging students and families. If school districts intend to reduce their out-of-district placements to therapeutic schools by serving students with similar profiles, the public school's program will need this same therapeutic structure in order to survive.

DOI: 10.4324/9781003270478-11

The word survive is used meaningfully, because without thoughtful support, the staff will burn out. The program will struggle to do quality work, out-of-district placements will continue, and the staff turnover will be so swift that the program will not have a meaningful core.

The therapeutic inclusion program offers a tremendous opportunity to help students and their families. The therapeutic work occurs in the milieu, in the general education environment, and in copious communication with parents. Operating in multiple roles at the intersection of these different elements, the work of the therapeutic inclusion program is in fact much more complex, generally speaking, than that of a therapist seeing individual clients in therapy. Furthermore, it is well understood in the mental health field that therapy without supervision is irresponsible practice (Haen & Aronson, 2017).

While no single element of the therapeutic inclusion program holds the whole system together, supervision is the connective tissue, the forum and the format, that allows the program to work with the distress and complexity over time (Haen & Aronson, 2017). A therapeutic inclusion program simply cannot be sustained without a strong supervision model in place.

The purposes of supervision

The therapeutic inclusion program is a psychodynamic program. In this context, this means the relationships themselves that exist within the program are the agents of change (Yalom, 2002), and the fundamental means of providing therapy to the students.

All those engaged in relationship-based therapeutic work naturally must bring themselves into the relationship. This leads to effective therapeutic work, while bringing up a number of factors for staff members that must be attended to carefully. For example: What parts of your authentic self are available for the therapeutic relationship? What parts of yourself are not? What are your blind spots in relationships? What are your heightened sensitivities? How is your own experience with family, school, and friends, impacting the way you are working with this group, in this school now? How are transference and countertransference playing out in your student and staff relationships?

Any of these questions, without being examined with support from a supervisor, could lead to the therapeutic work becoming ineffective and stuck, and to staff burnout.

The role of supervision in the therapeutic inclusion program

The role of the supervisor is multifaceted and adaptive to the evolving needs of the program. Supervision is a topic worthy of its own study and volumes. That being said, there are some elements of supervision that are worth highlighting in the context of the therapeutic inclusion program.

The supervisor's main aim is to support the purpose of the program, which is to provide the best therapeutic and educational care to the students who are members. The supervisor pursues this goal by supporting, guiding, and collaborating with staff who provide direct service. These therapeutic educators are the supervisees. The supervisor looks out for their well-being in their challenging work with children who sometimes experience significant and complex distress.

The supervisor does this through listening carefully, remaining attuned to their supervisees, bringing their own knowledge and experience into the conversation, and encouraging and offering insight into the work and dynamics at play. While there is an overlap in the approaches between supervision and therapy, the supervisor's scope is limited to the supervisee's relationship to their work in the program. There are factors from supervisee's lives outside of work that impact the way a supervisee sees and interacts with the therapeutic inclusion program. They are brought up in supervision as appropriate, with a focus always on supporting the supervisee in professional growth and doing their best work.

While feeling supported is a basic need in therapeutic work, therapeutic educators feel their best and do their best work when they are thriving. The supervisor should support their supervisees in their growth and development as therapeutic educators. In supervision, the work is discussed, interventions are designed, and decisions are made. The supervisor supports their supervisee's growth by helping to hold and think about challenging aspects of the work.

In a new supervisory relationship with a less-experienced supervisee, the supervisor may hold a significant amount of the responsibility around challenging and consequential decisions. During the supervision meeting, the supervisor models ways to approach challenging situations that need attention. Over the long term, there is a deliberate transfer of responsibility from the supervisor to the supervisee in terms of decision-making concerning their work. This supports the growth of the supervisee, strengthening the therapeutic inclusion program and helping the supervisee thrive.

This approach parallels the approach to group psychotherapy described in Chapter Three, where the counselor aims to calibrate their group management "just right" to allow the group to operate at their growing edge. In this approach, the management tasks left to the group are appropriately challenging—neither too easy, nor too difficult. Similarly, the supervisor calibrates their collaboration to allow their supervisees to operate at their growing edge, which leads to deep engagement and growth.

The supervisor models the unconditional positive regard, reliability, authentic relationship building, and creativity that is needed throughout the therapeutic inclusion program. Through this modeling, the supervisor has a significant hand in the nature and quality of the program's therapeutic culture (Nakkula & Ravitch, 1998).

Supervisory organization

The structure of supervision will largely depend on the relevant experience and development of the program counselor. Regardless of their levels of experience, the program co-leaders must be supervised by an experienced clinician, with experience specific to the work of therapeutic education. If the program counselor themselves has accumulated and integrated significant years of experience, they may in turn provide supervision to the rest of the therapeutic inclusion program staff. The experience of the program co-leader, the special education teacher, should also be taken into consideration. If the co-leadership team is not at a stage in their experience and development where they are ready to supervise the program staff, a program supervisor can support the program by assisting in supervision of the program staff.

A supervision model with a highly experienced program counselor

Supervision sessions should last a set time, with a range between 45 minutes and an hour being appropriate. It is an important distinction that supervision is not therapy, though there are some overlaps in the structure and approach. One similarity is that supervision meetings should begin and end on schedule. This is primarily the supervisor's responsibility, to be prepared and ready to meet on time, and also to hold the supervision space until the agreed upon ending time.

In this, and in all of the program supervisor's work, they are modeling quality therapeutic work for the program staff. Like group psychotherapy, supervision starts on time and ends on time to encourage a sense of security and predictability. The supervisor's timeliness is a message to the supervisees that they and their time are respected and valued, and that this meeting is important. Ending on time is a message of reliability and constancy. Additionally, in some cases there may be things that would benefit from discussion that the supervisor and supervisees are not aware of without time and space together to consider.

The therapeutic inclusion program co-leaders, the program counselor and special education teacher, must meet with their supervisor between 45 minutes and one hour weekly. As a leadership team, it is important that they attend this supervision meeting together.

The program counselor and special education teacher can then offer a group supervision to the rest of the staff that should again last between 45 minutes and an hour. The program counselor is responsible for fostering therapeutic thinking and support during the supervision, while the special education teacher co-leads as an equal partner, with an eye toward the academic needs of the students. However, it is important that members of the program do not feel confined to circumscribed roles compartmentalizing therapy and education. The relative expertise of individuals can be respected while a natural blending of ideas and perspectives occurs, just as a blending of therapy and academics is constantly occurring in the therapeutic milieu with students, as highlighted in Chapter Five.

A supervision model with a less experienced program counselor

If the program counselor is not highly experienced in therapeutic education, the program supervisor will take on a more active role in the program. It is particularly important in this case that the program supervisor is highly experienced in therapeutic education. They will supervise the program staff, but not work directly with students and families.

In this structure, the program supervisor will meet with the program co-leaders once a week for supervision and co-lead a meeting with the program co-leaders for the rest of the program staff once a week.

The program supervisor and administration

The program supervisor should have regular meetings with school administration, in order to help mediate between the varying needs of a public school and a specialized therapeutic program. Weekly meetings are likely not necessary, but regular meetings should be scheduled and a channel for communication must be open. The needs of a therapeutic inclusion program and the needs and norms of a public school are sometimes at odds. The therapeutic inclusion program approach is often foreign to the experience of public school administrators. They benefit from another source for therapeutic program understanding who is not directly enmeshed in the work with the students and families. The supervisor also will sometimes have to help the program co-leaders come to terms with the needs and limitations of the public school environment.

The program supervisor can help protect the relationship between the therapeutic inclusion program and the school administration by triangulating conflict. The program supervisor, not directly involved in the work with students nor directly involved with the administration, is well positioned to help hold the big picture and protect the therapeutic inclusion program's ability to do good work in the long term.

In order for the program supervisor to play this important role, they will need to have strong working relationships with the program co-leaders and with school administration. It is important to avoid a situation where the program supervisor can provide supervision, but is not in relationship with administration through regular communication. If this occurs, the supervisor may protect the program, but will not be able to mitigate between the sometimes differing expectations of a public school and a therapeutic inclusion program.

A supervision vignette from the East Classroom

It was a curious, lovely, and emotionally volatile group of seven students between the ages of 9 and 12 in the therapeutic milieu. This small group held a range of diagnoses and learning disabilities, including severe

ADHD, schizoaffective disorder, bipolar disorder, as well as students with unclear but developing diagnostic profiles.

Manuel was in his first year in the counselor role as program co-leader. He had been a paraprofessional for two years in the program while pursuing his degree in counseling. On many weekend nights, Manuel was a drummer in a jazz group that played regularly. His work as a paraprofessional was admired, and he was hired for the co-leader role after the position became available.

Manuel and his program co-leader Amy attended their weekly supervision meeting with their supervisor, Bridget. Bridget had significant experience in therapeutic work and in therapeutic education, working within the classroom-as-therapeutic-milieu model.

Manuel's partner Amy was a special education teacher, starting her fourth year in the co-leadership position. Through talent, and years of experience and supervision, she was very skilled in managing the milieu and helping the group regulate. However, this group was especially challenging behaviorally, and the necessities of Amy's schedule regularly left Manuel alone with the group.

During supervision, Manuel shared his frustration that the group struggled behaviorally when Amy was elsewhere. Also, he was not confident about his role within the balance of leadership during group psychotherapy. Amy had already co-led the group for three years and was accustomed to being in a leadership role during group psychotherapy. Now in the role of program counselor, Manuel felt a particular responsibility to take on more leadership during this time.

In her supervisory role, Bridget saw that the group needed Manuel to step more confidently into his role as co-leader. However, this would only support the program if Manuel could do so with authentic confidence. What was Manuel perhaps missing about himself that he could bring to the work for the benefit of the program? Supporting Manuel in understanding what he had to offer the program as an individual could bring him from insecurity to growth and thriving. This development would be of great value to the students in the program.

At a mid-October supervision, Bridget reminded Manuel that she had seen him play drums with his jazz group. He was a responsive and collaborative player. She had seen Manuel listening keenly to the others in his group, and responding with his approach to the drums. Manuel was getting out of the way for a developing solo one moment, taking up space to push the music forward at another, interacting lyrically with the soloist at another moment. All of this in response to both the individuals in the group and to the group expression. She told Manuel that his capacity to tune in and respond to the moment in the group was exactly the skill that Manuel needed in the milieu. As a drummer, he already knows how to do this. When visiting the classroom, Bridget had seen this same responsiveness during some of Manuel's best moments.

Bridget had to be patient with Manuel during supervision in his current state of insecurity in order for Manuel to consider what Bridget was putting forward. While Manuel remained resistant to the idea during the supervision session, the concept sank in over the ensuing days and weeks.

The idea stayed with Manuel. He took the analogy further, noticing in the milieu and during group psychotherapy that when the students were taking up social and emotional space in the room in a constructive way, he could take up less space. Alternately, when an individual or the group was radiating distress in a way that could gain momentum in the group, Manuel could use his personality to take up more space. In the moment, he could play his friendly personality like a big drum solo if it helped the group avoid getting caught up in an individual student's distress. And while Manuel took up space, the student in distress could get support from another staff member, or might tune into what Manuel was offering.

The highly integrated nature of the elements of the therapeutic inclusion program allow positive interventions to support the program through multiple levels. Bridget's personalized metaphor in supervision had supported Manuel's growth. This growth led to an improvement in the emotional/behavioral temperature of the therapeutic milieu. Additionally, Bridget had modeled the use of unconditional positive regard in a relationship-based, personalized intervention that highlighted knowing and seeing the individual she was seeking to assist. These are exactly the valuable tools that Manuel and Amy would use in their ongoing work with their students.

Manuel continued to grow his ability to tune in and be responsive to both individuals and the group in the milieu. Each workday provided the space and time to develop this ability. Group psychotherapy, an approach which emphasizes the importance of here and now, provided an especially rich environment for Manuel to use his developing skills to step into co-leadership with Amy.

Conclusion

Regular and well-integrated supervision is a mandatory component of the therapeutic inclusion program. The therapeutic inclusion program is a relationship-based, psychodynamically oriented approach. It exists to serve the needs of students with significant social, emotional, and behavioral difficulties, for whom more standardized behavior-based interventions have not been or would not be effective. Supervision enables and sustains this challenging and rewarding undertaking.

Unfortunately, the use of supervision is counter to trends in public school counseling, where it has been excised from therapeutic work in many school districts. This is bad practice in general and is absolutely not an option for the therapeutic inclusion program.

References

Haen, C., & Aronson, S. (2017). *Handbook of child and adolescent group therapy: A practitioner's reference*. Routledge.

Nakkula, M. J., & Ravitch, S. M. (1998). *Matters of interpretation: Reciprocal transformation in therapeutic and developmental relationships with youth*. Jossey-Bass.

Yalom, I. (2002). *The gift of therapy*. HarperCollins.

11 A Resilient Structure Part Three

The Role of Administrators

The school administration completes the truss that supports the therapeutic inclusion program. By working with the program staff and program supervision, the trio of support beams reinforce each other. With this structure the school can sustain the complex, intense, and rewarding work of the therapeutic inclusion program.

Other books aim to comprehensively prepare school administrators for their roles. This chapter guides administrators in how to best work with and support the therapeutic inclusion program. This chapter looks at the benefits of having a therapeutic inclusion program, from an administrative level. It explains the administrator's important role in the program, and why an informed administration is integral to the program's health and maintenance. A vignette drawn from a formative therapeutic inclusion program experience reinforces the important role of administrators.

The key role of the administration is to act as a protective roof over the program. The administration is naturally responsible for looking out for the school community at large. This positions the administrator well to take into account the big picture, the longer term, and to make difficult decisions among sometimes competing interests.

There is a parallel to the parental role in the administrative role that a therapeutic practitioner will recognize. Like a parent considering the long-term needs of their family, the administrator must weigh and balance a larger range of concerns and interests across their school or district when working with the therapeutic inclusion program. Sometimes the administrator must deliver unwelcome news about what cannot be done, and what must be done. The effective administrator is always looking out for the best interests of the program, within the context of the larger educational system for which they are responsible.

School and district wide effects of an effective therapeutic inclusion program

The positive effects of an effective therapeutic inclusion program go well beyond the direct recipients of the program's services. A quality therapeutic inclusion program can provide budget relief by decreasing out-of-district

DOI: 10.4324/9781003270478-12

placements. While the cost of an out-of-district tuition alone is enormous, the cost of transportation is also considerable, and there are other significant expenses if there is legal activity around the placement. For example, based on data publicly available through the Massachusetts Operational Services Division (2022) the average annual tuition of an approved Massachusetts in-state private special education program for 2023 is $146,409. When residential programs are excluded, average tuition for 2023 is $90,515. These figures do not include transportation costs, a significant additional expense that the district usually must pay. A therapeutic inclusion program is also expensive to operate, but can result in significant savings in reducing out-of-district placements.

Keeping students in-district has benefits well beyond budgetary. When program students remain in their home community, it is meaningful that they are *included*. While the students and families themselves experience this deeply, so does the community around them. The inclusion embraces diversity and prepares all students in the community for a world where a wider range of neurodiversity and mental health realities are acknowledged and integrated into daily living.

The therapeutic inclusion program also influences the culture of the school at large. The program demonstrates and shares a relationship and empathy-based approach with the rest of the community, especially in the program's work supporting teachers and students in the general education environments. The collaborative nature of the therapeutic inclusion program provides general education teachers with new approaches and perspectives. While working together, the general education teachers integrate creative, relationship-based, behaviorally informed approaches into their work. This leads to a richer, deeper, and more rewarding experience for the classroom, and is an experience general education teachers can carry forward through their career.

The Social Emotional Learning (SEL) movement gathered momentum in the mid 2010s. The educational community's understanding of the importance of SEL has only grown, and now is a central school and classroom consideration. The research consensus holds that emphasizing SEL has significant well-being and academic benefits, and that the positive impact on learning outmatches the results of putting resources on other emphases (Mahoney et al., 2018).

The therapeutic inclusion program serves as an SEL leader and laboratory within the school district. The demands of the program students and families prioritize social and emotional concerns, forming the program staff into resident SEL experts. The staff develops the kind of expertise that only arrives when one must consider SEL concerns of significant consequence constantly while at work. As we often see in work within autism spectrum disorder and attention deficit hyperactivity disorder communities, the supports that are helpful to students with diagnoses are often very helpful to students who do not have disability diagnoses. Trends that have expanded from the special education community to general usage include weighted blankets, fidgets, chewies, and routine schedule previewing. Similarly within the school district, the therapeutic inclusion program becomes a positive SEL influence and model, as well as a resource for consultation.

Protecting therapeutic relationships

The therapeutic inclusion program will require relationships with administrators ranging from the school principal or principal team and special education coordinator, to the special education director, the superintendent, and the school board or committee. As high-level administrators, the school board, superintendent, and special education director will not be apprised of the daily operations of the program. However, it is important that the therapeutic inclusion program has support at the highest levels of administration, given the complex and sensitive work at hand. It is generally the roles of the building principal or special education coordinator, chiefly whichever building administrator is designated as building level point person, and program supervisor (as discussed in Chapter Ten), to maintain these relationships with the higher administration.

Within the therapeutic model, the attending administrator must appreciate the importance of therapeutic relationships and be prepared to protect them. As a relationship-based program, meaningful working relationships are formed with students and parents. The therapeutic work takes place within these relationships. This experience of working collaboratively to address the needs of the student is mostly one of mutual appreciation for the good work that occurs. Positive feelings often flow naturally in these relationships. Under the care of the therapeutic educators and the supervision process, these interpersonal connections mostly protect and sustain themselves.

However, in the course of their work, all educators will at times encounter difficult relationships with parents. Due to the complex and often previously misunderstood needs of their child, some parents approach their relationship with the school with a range of emotions and hesitation. This may come across as an antagonistic or contentious style of relating. Additionally, like any group of people, some parents have mental health issues that impact their interpersonal style. These parents and their children need therapeutic support as much, if not more, than any other families.

Within these relationships between parents and the therapeutic inclusion program, the program co-leader managing communication with home is the initial point of contact for the distress the family is experiencing. At times, this person can become the target of the parent's distress. In this circumstance the resilient truss consisting of staff, supervisory, and administrative support must bear weight. If the truss is not activated at these times, the therapeutic relationships are at risk. The child's ability to receive the best care will be in jeopardy. Staff, administration, and supervision must collaborate with responsive and thoughtful care to the distress of a parent or parent team. If not, instead of feeling cared for by a cohesive school and home collaboration, the student can feel as if they need to pick sides. The distressed adult relationships enter the milieu and can have a spillover effect on the entire program. To be clear, as described in Chapter Eight, the goal is not to create relationships free from distress, but to use the program to support relationships that can withstand and contain distress when it arrives.

In order to protect the therapeutic relationships, the therapeutic educator turns to their supervisor for support and guidance. The therapeutic educator and supervisor may then turn toward the administrator to protect the therapeutic relationship. The administrator responds by responding to parent concerns, and establishing and reinforcing appropriate boundaries when necessary. This is difficult work, but similar to an invested parent protecting a family member, a supportive administrator protects the relationships between staff and parents. The administrator does this because the therapeutic alliance between the program staff and the student's parents is an essential element of the therapeutic work.

The goal is always to maintain trusting collaborative relationships within the therapeutic inclusion program, based on the common interest of everyone involved to be of service to the student's healthy development. This requires flexibility, creativity, and boundary maintenance. In some instances, the administrator may have to play a similar role with school staff.

Protecting the therapeutic inclusion program in the context of the school community

The administrator protects the therapeutic program's relationship with students, families, and other school employees. For example, the administrator can take responsibility for a programming decision that a parent or colleague finds unfavorable, especially if the decision has an administrative basis.

Administrators naturally have more of the bird's eye view, and relationships throughout district levels and departments. The administrator protects the program by helping to make the best hires, partnering the program with the most appropriate general education teachers, and at times limiting how the program can operate due to the administrator's larger scope of the school system. In these ways the administration acts as a protective roof over the therapeutic inclusion program.

An informed administration

The program requires a point person or team from the administrative hierarchy who is kept well-informed with weekly meetings. In most cases, these administrators are the school principal, assistant principal, and/or special education coordinator. These key administrators are part of the therapeutic inclusion program and part of the district administration. While maintaining appropriate confidentiality boundaries, it is important that this administrator be an informed partner in the operation of the program. The program co-leaders, as well as the program supervisor, will continuously update this administrator on what the program is doing and why.

As a program which encourages creativity, staff should carefully avoid the administration being surprised or uninformed about developments. The administrator must also have a voice in the creative process, particularly as resources or competing interests may require the administrator to redirect or limit interventions.

Budgetary concerns

The budget represents the scarce resource with which the district seeks to thoughtfully care for their students, understandably making the budget a central and recurring concern. School boards and committees, superintendents, special education directors, and other administrators are always looking for opportunities to use the budget more efficiently. The therapeutic inclusion program is a significant expense and can get the attention of an administrator or school board member on a spreadsheet. However, this figure must be compared to the cost of likely out-of-district placements. Once a therapeutic inclusion program is in place, some administrators may believe they can replace it with a leaner, less relationship-based and more data-driven, behaviorist model. What they do not account for is that if these behaviorist models worked for all students, there would be no need for out-of-district placements to schools with more comprehensive approaches, and no need for a therapeutic inclusion program.

A behavioral model can be leaner than a therapeutic inclusion program and is effective for some students. However, a behavioral model will not address the therapeutic needs underpinning the behavioral issues. Furthermore, there will always be a population of students for whom behavior-based interventions will never be effective, without copious therapeutic support.

The trend toward data-driven approaches has benefits and can lead to nimble administrations that are able to integrate new information and make positive change. Alongside the movement toward data collection in education, there is currently a simultaneous trend toward relationship-based work, often under the SEL heading. Quality SEL initiatives reap tremendous benefits that cannot all be reflected in a data set.

Many districts have relatively rapid turnover on their school boards and upper administration, leading to myopic strategy and a lack of institutional history and character. For example, one school district in Massachusetts reached out to a colleague about starting a therapeutic inclusion program, unaware that the district had previously collaborated with that professional to establish and maintain a therapeutic inclusion program over the course of 14 years. That program had been discontinued by a short-sighted superintendent eight years prior. The latest superintendent picked up the phone to reach out to the same professional, with no knowledge of their district's prior 14-year collaboration with him.

A formative experience with the integral role of administration

Sometime after my experience in a private therapeutic school, I (Michael Murray) accepted a role working with a very small group of students in a public school setting. While the plan was to start a therapeutic program, the staff at this point consisted of only myself and a paraprofessional. During this experience, without a defined support structure, the need for the three support beams of program staff, supervision, and administration became clear. I wrote a memo to the school principal and the school counselor (whom I had asked to supervise me) to describe the support that was needed in order to contain and withstand the distress developing in a difficult staff and parent relationship.

I titled it "The Cost of a Therapeutic Program," as a play on the word "cost." Administrators must attend to financial concerns. However, the real challenge of sustaining a therapeutic inclusion program is receiving, holding, and processing the distress of students and families that are struggling with significant social, emotional, and behavioral difficulties. (Some modifications have been made to the letter for the purposes of this chapter.)

The Cost of a Therapeutic Program

Our recent experiences in the maturation of our still-so-young therapeutic program have me thinking about learning from experience, and what our program will need in order to grow both sturdy and effective. In order to think through it, I come back to the beginning: why did we start the program? My understanding is that we started it because we wanted to help families stay in the local community, while they receive the services the students and families need to make their school experience work.

That leads to the questions: why do families facing behavioral and psychological challenges look for out-of-district placements? What are they looking for that was not provided in the public school system? I don't think it's any particular set of services. The schools they go to are typically therapeutic schools.

I believe that what a good therapeutic school offers, which the typical elementary school may not, is the ability to receive, absorb, process, and diffuse throughout the structure, the deep emotional pain the families are in. There is a grieving process that comes along with parents coming to terms with the intense and unanticipated emotional and behavioral disturbances experienced by their child. The parents have to rethink their whole vision of childhood, the whole future they anticipated for their child, and the whole rest of their own lives.

The pain they are experiencing is in many cases beyond what parents can contain and process on their own. The overflow is likely to manifest in any number of ways, often including resentment toward those who are helping (the nearest logical receivers). Whatever the case, the people who make up the therapeutic program are going to be in a position to accept their pain. This is part of the therapeutic process, and it is something that a program organized around behaviorism is unlikely to provide. We accept their pain in two connotations of the word *accept.* We accept its validity without diminishing it or turning away. And by doing so we, in a small but significant way, accept (co-experience) their pain.

Structure

Weight and structure become useful metaphors for how we can accept, diffuse, and process the emotional content we will be lifting with families. One pillar can hold up some weight. Two can hold up more. And three can be arranged in a triangle of mutually supporting pieces, which can sustain much more weight. Similarly, we are finding our structure as a group of professionals in this program, and how to diffuse the weight so that our structure can stand under pressure.

In relationship-based therapeutic work, the therapeutic teacher holds the students in relationship. The therapeutic teacher provides and enforces the boundaries of the relationship, while remaining consistently available and seeking to empathetically understand, throughout the student's ups and downs. The therapeutic teacher also has a therapeutic relationship with the parents, maintained through the daily communication book, and weekly phone calls.

If the boundaries of a parent–teacher relationship were crossed by a parent, or if levels of acrimony were concerning, interventions may require an administrator to intervene with the parent. Internally, they might explain they were taking it on in order to preserve the teacher–parent therapeutic relationship—true enough. But perhaps the structure and weight metaphor is even more apt. By listening responsively while reinforcing boundaries or expectations, the administrator is drawing off some of the emotional pain of the parent, and that administrator is likely to receive a share of the parent's emotional weight. In many cases, the parents may very well redirect their resentment toward the administrator. No matter how tough we may feel ourselves to be, this experience is difficult for anyone. However, diffusing the weight in this way allows the structure to stand, and for the therapeutic teacher to continue their work with the family.

That's why I gave this piece of writing this title. I was thinking that accepting the emotional weight—the pain, of the families we will help, is the true cost of having a therapeutic program. And that is why I wrote this piece. If I could have articulated it better from the start, I would have. Everyone in the program's support structure should understand this important piece of their role. Part of the weight at times is going to reach the most empowered individual position in the district, the superintendent. But most of the time, the program staff, supervisor, and principal will be able to diffuse the weight and hold the structure.

Our early and rich opportunities to learn from our experiences in our new program, and the mirrored experience of our families as they encounter new challenges and wish for quick fixes, have me thinking about a favorite passage in W.R. Bion's 1961 book, *Experiences in Groups.* Bion was a psychiatrist and early formulator of group psychotherapy. I include this as the equivalent of a pep-talk on the value of learning through experience. I know I need it, at least. Bion writes this under the heading: *THE HATRED OF LEARNING BY EXPERIENCE*

> There is a hatred of having to learn by experience at all, and lack of faith in the worth of such a kind of learning. A little experience of groups soon shows that this is not simply a negative attitude; the process of development is really being compared with some other state, that nature of which is not immediately apparent. The belief in this other state often shows itself in everyday life, perhaps most clearly in the schoolboy belief in the hero who never does any work but is always in top form … In the group it becomes very clear that this longed-for alternative to [learning from experience] is really something like arriving fully equipped as an adult fitted by instinct to know without training or development exactly how to live and move and have his being in a group.
>
> (p. 89)

Conclusion

The administration is a fundamental part of the structure that sustains the therapeutic inclusion program. The district administration should be represented by one or two administrators who attend weekly meetings with the program co-leaders in order to remain informed and to collaborate with the therapeutic inclusion program. These administrators are part of the therapeutic inclusion program and the district administration. As such, they act as a liaison between the two entities. They bring their experience, creativity, and administrative perspective into their work with the therapeutic inclusion program. These building-based administrators will do the great majority of administrative work with, and supporting, the therapeutic inclusion program. We include the whole district administration as part of the program structure however, because the building administrators work must be backed by the district administration in order to be effective.

While the administrator brings their creativity and knowledge into the collaboration, their role is primarily protective. The program staff works directly with the students and parents, and the staff turns toward supervision for support and therapeutic planning. The administration protects the program by bringing a bird's-eye view to the needs of the therapeutic inclusion program and the school as scarce resources are allocated, and any competing interests are negotiated.

At higher levels of the administration, all the way through school board or committee, administrators and the program supervisor maintain relationships to ensure that the program is understood, and that the program has therapeutically expert representation at the highest levels.

References

Bion, W. R. (1961). *Experiences in groups and other papers*. Routledge.

Commonwealth of Massachusetts. (2022, February 11). *In State FY 2023 special education programs – mass.gov*. Mass.gov. Retrieved April 12, 2022, from www.mass.gov/doc/in-state-special-education-fy23/download

Mahoney, J. L., Durlak, J. A., & Weissberg, R. P. (2018). An update on social and emotional learning outcome research. *Phi Delta Kappan*, 100(4), 18–23.

12 Conclusion

Integrating Parts into a Whole

Our work in a therapeutic inclusion program is a process of integration. Students and families often arrive reporting previous experiences of chaos and frustration. We help our students and families integrate their past, present, and ongoing experience. When students experience school failure, it is rarely contained in school. The trickle-down, or more likely, the snowball effect of their difficulties at school is felt at home within the family.

The therapeutic inclusion program works to create a narrative that uplifts students and creates a model of collaboration between home and school. This, of course, does not mean that students in the program will never experience difficulty. The difficulty is inevitable. What it does mean is that there will be a relationship in place between the program staff and the family that is prepared to hold the student's distress.

The concluding chapter brings together elements of the therapeutic inclusion program in a narrative from our experience demonstrating how the relationships between student, staff, and family can develop profoundly for the benefit of the child. The chapter also reinforces that the program is not a set of strategies or solutions, but rather is a collaborative and therapeutic structure where reparative relationships develop, and creativity supported through supervision leads to individualized interventions. In the school environment where students, staff, and administrators are so often expected to have the answers, the therapeutic inclusion program is an oasis that can tolerate not-knowing.

A different kind of communication

In responding to challenging behaviors at school, collaboration through the program staff is fundamentally different from typical disciplinary communication provided by the school's administration. Though well-meaning, this type of communication via the principal or assistant principal often leaves parents feeling as though their child has behaved badly. For our students with significant social and emotional challenges, planning for reparation, repair, and moving forward is often insufficient. The school's administration does not have the relationships, time, or expertise required to respond with thoughtful care and attunement.

DOI: 10.4324/9781003270478-13

Through the relationship-based approach of the therapeutic inclusion program, families are able to hear missteps and difficult times that occur at school, as they are communicated alongside the progress and celebrations. The program staff's ability to listen to families with the intent to understand and truly partner over the success of their children is consistently well-received. Collaboration with families to address challenges in both the home and school environments is vital for holding the student. The developing narrative can reflect a positive trajectory given the support and insight available through the relationships between the program, the students, the teachers, and the family.

Families who have had previous difficult or failed relationships with school staff find themselves listened to, understood, and supported through the program. This integration for the child, referred to as "home and school working together" (Reinstein, 2006), is vital. The following vignette highlights how this communication, fully supporting both families and the student, paves the way for student success.

Gabriel

Gabriel's family lived in a town with a school district that afforded them school choice at the elementary level. The school system had various educational programs housed in their elementary schools including an autism program, a language-based learning disability program, a life skills program, and a therapeutic inclusion program.

Starting school in the district—kindergarten

Gabriel's family were immigrants and English language learners. They made their school choice based solely on proximity to their home. The school that Gabriel chose housed the life skills program, though this was not a determining factor for their family in choosing an elementary school.

Gabriel began kindergarten and had a challenging transition into school. He had difficulty following teacher-directed plans. Forming relationships with his peers also proved to be difficult. Gabriel had no previous school experience and was learning English, as his family spoke Portuguese in the home. These factors were important to take into consideration as transitioning to an English-speaking, full-day kindergarten was a significant shift for Gabriel. Gabriel's teacher continued to support him throughout kindergarten, yet remained concerned about his presentation.

At times, Gabriel would exhibit atypical levels of aggression with his peers. Though this was rare, it felt concerning to his teacher. At times these bouts of aggression would come from predictable events, such as someone cheating at a soccer game at recess. Other times they felt wholly unpredictable, as though they had come from nowhere. Gabriel's teacher,

Ms. Jones, brought him to the school's child study team in November, and again in February. In addition to his aggressive episodes, Gabriel also presented with pervasive difficulty learning throughout the day. He struggled to attend to lessons. Ms. Jones was not sure whether this was due to his EL status, a lack of prior knowledge, difficulty with the curriculum, a lack of motivation, or some combination.

When Gabriel would engage in aggressive episodes at school Ms. Jones would call home and speak to his mother ("to" and not "with" is a meaningful distinction here). Though Gabriel lived with both parents, his mother was the primary contact to the school. These conversations, in part due to a language barrier, were difficult. Though Ms. Jones was thoughtful in providing behavior-based retellings of the events that occurred, it was difficult for Gabriel's mother, Ana, to hear. She would apologize for his behavior, and offer to speak to him at home, though neither Ms. Jones nor Ana felt much confidence about how to help Gabriel avoid these episodes. Ms. Jones did not ask Ana about how Gabriel was doing at home, or if any of these challenges existed in that environment as well. Ms. Jones was already pushed to her limits in the demanding role of general education kindergarten teacher and was not able to engage in any long or significant conversations with Ana.

As spring came, Gabriel began having increasing difficulty in school. He had mostly stopped engaging in academic work in his classroom, and he was becoming increasingly disruptive. Gabriel would stand on chairs and tables, throw and rip his work, and refuse to complete most activities. One day at recess, another child called Gabriel a cheater when he was playing a game of soccer, and Gabriel responded by throwing him to the ground and punching him. At this point the school's principal, Ms. Howe, called Ana. Ana viewed a disciplinary call from the principal of the school as very serious. She took this to mean that Gabriel was in trouble. Ana wanted to help Gabriel be successful at school, but she did not know how. She worried that Gabriel may be suspended or kicked out of school, and the language barrier and her anxiety made it difficult to engage in productive and meaningful conversation with Ms. Howe.

Throughout the remainder of the school year, Gabriel continued to present similarly. Incidents of aggression were periodic, and he continued to have difficulty attending in the classroom and was distracting to his peers. Gabriel began to develop a view of himself as being a "bad boy" and had determined that he hated school and that he was "bad at school." Ms. Howe took over communication with Ana for difficult events, and Ms. Jones called with less difficult updates, though there was very limited positive communication delivered at this point. Neither Ms. Howe nor Ms. Jones felt as though they had hopeful messages to convey. The school was left wondering whether Gabriel's EL and kindergarten status were the determining factors in his presentation at school, or whether there were other factors that they were not yet aware of. In April, the school decided to do a full battery of special education testing to gather more information. Ana was happy to allow the school to complete special education testing, hoping that the results would provide guidance and support for Gabriel.

The testing showed that Gabriel needed specialized instruction in reading, writing, math, as well as speech and language and occupational therapy. He also received consultation services with the school district's BCBA and check-ins with the school counselor, as needed. Due to his range of needs and his age, Gabriel was diagnosed by the school as having a developmental delay. He would also continue to receive English language services.

As he had not previously received any special education services, it was determined that Gabriel's placement would stay in his current elementary school. The hope was that by addressing his learning, speech, and occupational therapy deficits as well as providing periodic counseling and positive behavior supports, Gabriel would be less frustrated and more successful in his current school environment.

First grade

Gabriel finished his kindergarten year, attended extended school year with similar presentation, and began his first-grade year with Ms. Carlton. Ms. Carlton welcomed Gabriel into her classroom, but soon became overwhelmed by his presence. Ms. Carlton recognized that Gabriel had a disability, yet could not sufficiently adjust her expectations to fit his presentation. This potential teacher/student mismatch, along with the increasing work demands of first grade, led to an incredibly difficult start to the year for Gabriel. In addition to work refusal and distracting behavior in the classroom, Gabriel had a significant uptick in his aggression both in frequency and intensity. Multiple times per week, Gabriel would agress at students and now staff. His behavior warranted a placement discussion.

As the therapeutic inclusion program was housed at a different elementary school than Gabriel's current placement, the entry criteria were reviewed by his IEP team. Gabriel met the first three eligibility criteria: (1) the child must have a disability and be found eligible for special education services in order to join the Therapeutic Inclusion Program; (2) the student should be diagnosed with an emotional disability, including developmental delay; and (3) interventions such as behavior intervention plans, created in consultation with the district BCBA, and other less-restrictive interventions (relative to joining the Therapeutic Inclusion Program) have been thoroughly tried, and have been determined to be insufficiently effective by the IEP team toward maintaining appropriate progress through the curriculum.

The therapeutic inclusion program's therapist, Mr. Twomey, conducted two observations of Gabriel. Through these observations Mr. Twomey made some recommendations to Gabriel's plan, though also recommended that the current setting could not provide the therapeutic environment that would afford Gabriel the opportunity to truly thrive. The IEP team reconvened, and a placement in the Oak Program was recommended, which was fully endorsed by Gabriel's family who were willing to accept any help that the school was able to provide. Then a transition plan was made.

Transition to the therapeutic inclusion program

As the therapeutic inclusion program was housed in a different elementary school than Gabriel attended, he would need to transfer elementary schools in order to access the program. While a change in placement often creates anxiety, a transition was especially delicate for Gabriel as his experiences in kindergarten and first grade did not provide him with many positive associations with school and learning. He had social difficulties throughout and viewed himself as a failure at school. By attending a new school, where he could be part of a therapeutic milieu with skilled staff, there was an opportunity for Gabriel to rebuild his school experience positively.

In order to facilitate a successful transition, both for Gabriel and the other students in the Oak Program, the change needed to be carefully thought out and previewed. Social stories were written for both Gabriel and the group. The co-leaders of the Oak Program, Mr. Twomey and special education teacher Mrs. Tabor, came to visit Gabriel at his current school with the hope of beginning to form a relationship. This occurred during preferred times of the day for Gabriel to increase the odds of starting with positive encounters. The program co-leaders came with carefully selected toys and books, showing interest in Gabriel. During these times, the social stories that had been written were read to Gabriel and then sent home, including a copy in Portuguese, so that he could experience them with his family as well. Mrs. Tabor and Mr. Twomey came with the message that they were interested in Gabriel. They knew that school had been hard. It was their job to help understand why and be helpful, and they had the means to do so.

During this time the Oak therapist, Mr. Twomey, who would be Gabriel's primary contact at school, developed a relationship with the family. Weekly phone calls were established where Mr. Twomey and Ana could begin to form an open and mutually respectful relationship. Gabriel's father Rodrigo was consistently invited to the conversation, though typically declined given his work schedule.

Ana quickly recognized these phone calls as beneficial and productive. This was different from her previous experience of receiving calls only when a behavioral issue had occurred at school, followed by trying her best to remedy the situation from home without significant home–school collaboration. Her weekly calls with Mr. Twomey had a very different flavor. Mr. Twomey was calling in order to hear and understand Ana's experience with Gabriel at home. He wanted to gain an understanding of Ana's expertise surrounding her child and create a secure partnership for Gabriel.

Gabriel's transition into the Oak classroom went as expected by the program staff. He started by visiting the classroom with just the program co-leaders present, Mr. Twomey and Mrs. Tabor, followed by a visit to morning circle—the program morning ritual that would orient Gabriel to each school day. After incrementally increased visits, Gabriel made a full switch to his new school.

Gabriel did not have a seamless transition into the therapeutic inclusion program, as he was coming from an experience of significant school failure. However, he was met in the Oak milieu with unconditional positive regard, a welcoming physical space, and a staff who could contain Gabriel's distress. Access to the program helped move Gabriel's difficulty from the general education environment, placing it within the therapeutic inclusion program classroom which was better suited to meet it. Relatively quickly, Gabriel learned that the Oak room was a place he could safely have "big feelings." Confident there was a safe space to go when triggered or escalated, Gabriel experienced less anxiety encountering the sometimes overwhelming demands of the first-grade environment.

Simultaneously, Gabriel was building a reparative relationship with Mr. Twomey. This relationship was invaluable for Gabriel. Mr. Twomey continued to develop a working relationship with Ana that supported Gabriel between home and school. This was a new and powerful experience for Gabriel. Within this web of connected care, Gabriel was held and seen as his whole authentic self.

Despite the care that Gabriel was given, school was still difficult for him. Gabriel still had learning, speech, and occupational therapy-related challenges. However, within the confines of the therapeutic milieu, these issues could be approached in a different way.

Learning to read in the therapeutic inclusion program classroom

Gabriel's difficulty learning to read was causing him significant distress. Gabriel presented as a student with a specific learning disability in reading, but paired with his emotional challenges, reading instruction had proved to be near impossible thus far, and this was causing him profound distress. Gabriel had determined that he was "stupid" in reading and that his teacher also thought that he was stupid because he had to do the same things "over and over and over again." Though learning to read in the initial stages does call for significant repetition, it was clear to Mrs. Tabor that a creative solution was required.

Gabriel was very interested in anime and graphic novels, but he was not ready to read complex texts. He was still working on letter sound correspondence and basic sight reading words. Mrs. Tabor found that in order to engage Gabriel in reading instruction they had to start each daily reading lesson with a break where they could strengthen their relationship through playing together. From there, they would do some reading from a preferred graphic novel. In fact, Mrs. Tabor put forth significant work procuring coveted graphic novels from local libraries as well as previewing the books for school-appropriate content. Her effort to obtain reading content that was interesting to Gabriel was not lost on him. He noticed the care that his teacher provided in helping him learn to read.

After spending some time listening to the graphic novel, hunting for words that he could read, and having comprehension conversations about the text, more traditional first-grade reading instruction could begin. In small doses, with a visual checklist of tasks, and earning another reinforcing break at the end, Gabriel began to attend to instruction and made significant progress. This progress helped him to feel more successful as a reader, building his confidence and momentum.

This is not to say that reading instruction was consistently successful. There were still days when Gabriel could not access the curriculum or attend to Mrs. Tabor. He would yell at her that he was stupid, and that she thought he was stupid. He would hide under the table or, when especially upset, kick around a few objects in the classroom. Mrs. Tabor continued to hold Gabriel in positive regard throughout. It was clear to the Oak team that even on days when he could not access instruction Gabriel was always doing his best. This message was clearly and consistently passed along to Gabriel. Sometimes, he was able to hear it.

Developing self-regulation

Previously, Gabriel would escalate violently, attacking peers and adults with the intent to harm. Through significant work in a reparative relationship with Mr. Twomey, Gabriel named the behavior "flying off the handle." When in a calm state, he could recognize that flying off the handle felt terrible. It was not something that he wanted to do. Gabriel wanted help with this, and the program staff was ready to help. Over time it was observed that when Gabriel was about to fly off the handle, conversation was not helpful. Efforts at verbal de-escalation were counterproductive. He found quiet time to himself more effective. Gabriel would go to the cozy corner and let the program staff know when he was ready to talk. Almost all of the time, Gabriel was able to use this routine to process and move on.

When in the cozy corner, Gabriel could be observed shaking with anger, often resulting in tears before he would call a trusted program staff member over to help him. At one point, Mr. Twomey commented that "seeing you cry, you look like the bravest person I could imagine. Not flying off the handle and controlling your anger is so strong and so brave." This statement resonated with Gabriel. He loved superheroes, and was ready to understand strength and courage in a more sophisticated way.

During meeting (group psychotherapy), Gabriel emerged over time as a humble leader. He demonstrated self-regulation under difficult circumstances, while maintaining understanding and empathy for students who were not able to do so as consistently.

Though Gabriel continued to have aggressive episodes at times, they became few and far between. He began to access the curriculum. He viewed himself as a "very smart math student." The reparative relationships and work done within the therapeutic milieu helped Gabriel to reframe his view of himself as a learner. After establishing healing relationships within the program, he made a deep and connected relationship with his general education teacher. He carried with him the ability to calm himself, or exit situations to a safe and reliable place. His developing self-regulation allowed him to enjoy rowdy and fun soccer matches with his classmates at recess. Gabriel's family received positive messages from school, contributing to a shared sense of forward momentum in his progress. Gabriel's mother and father shared back about successful times at home between Gabriel and his little brother. Gabriel was truly able to be held and thrive within the therapeutic inclusion program.

Concluding, beginning, and not-knowing

Schools are a place where knowledge is stored, sought, and gained. The children are there to learn. The adults are there to teach. This is a simplistic description. Still, the undercurrent of this simple understanding is always present. Teachers, staff, and administrators all feel pressure to know their stuff, to know what to do, to know what will solve the problem presented. Teachers have specific and effective educational and behavioral interventions that can be implemented, which are very effective when applied to the right situation. A sharp professional can often see the issues, use appropriate evaluation tools, and implement an effective intervention.

Students who require a therapeutic inclusion program usually have not sufficiently had their needs met through this approach. The puzzle presented is perhaps richer and calls for time and patience. The therapeutic program staff starts not only with forming relationships, but also with not-knowing. The staff, with support from supervision, can stay with not-knowing, as the relationships and the understanding unfolds. In the space between a growing understanding and not-knowing, the creativity and care within the staff–student–parent relationships begins to bridge the gap.

The therapeutic inclusion program at the city or town level is a solution to the district's struggles to provide in-district education for students with significant social, emotional, and behavioral difficulties. On the program level, the therapeutic inclusion program is less a solution, and instead a safe and reliable structure for creativity and care. The program creates a structure and space that are connected and related enough to safely not-know together. Within this patient, responsive, and relationship-based space, caring and effective responses are developed using psychological and pedagogical principles, all within a highly collaborative therapeutic structure.

This book concludes, paradoxically, with the intention of welcoming educators and counselors to tolerate the unresolved stories of their students and families facing significant social, emotional, and behavioral challenges. This book is a guide and an invitation to create a collaborative structure where staff, parents, and students can safely not-know together, while beginning to understand.

Reference

Reinstein, D. K. (2006). *To hold and be held: The therapeutic school as a holding environment.* Routledge.

Appendices

Appendix A

Oak entry criteria

The Oak Program is a therapeutic inclusion program designed to support students with social/emotional disabilities who require modification and support beyond what can be provided in the general education environment. Students are provided with accommodations, modifications, services support models, and individual behavior support plans all while being monitored and adjusted individually over time.

- The child must have a disability and be found eligible for special education services in order to join the Oak Program.
- The student should be diagnosed with an emotional disability, including developmental delay.
- Interventions such as behavior intervention plans, created in consultation with the district BCBA, and other less-restrictive interventions have been thoroughly tried and documented, and have been determined by the IEP team to be insufficiently effective in maintaining appropriate progress through the curriculum.
- If the previous criteria are satisfied, a staff member from the Oak Program is to perform an observation of the student, and make recommendations. If adjustments to the child's current program are agreed based on the observations and recommendations, they should be implemented. In order to be placed in the Oak Program, these adjustments must be implemented and deemed ineffective by the team.
- The last criteria, if all other criteria are satisfied, is that the IEP team agrees through consensus that the Oak Program is likely to be effective in supporting the student toward progress through the curriculum.

Appendix B

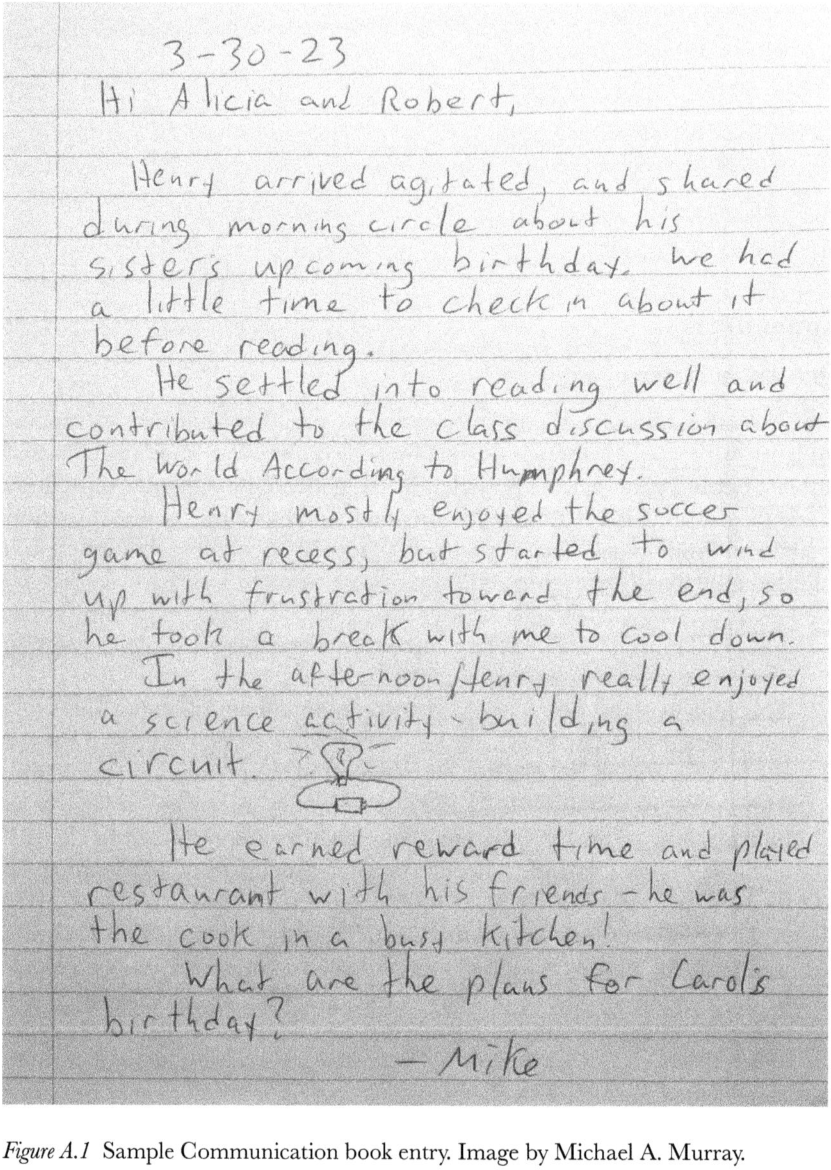

3-30-23

Hi Alicia and Robert,

Henry arrived agitated, and shared during morning circle about his sister's upcoming birthday. We had a little time to check in about it before reading.

He settled into reading well and contributed to the class discussion about The World According to Humphrey.

Henry mostly enjoyed the soccer game at recess, but started to wind up with frustration toward the end, so he took a break with me to cool down.

In the afternoon Henry really enjoyed a science activity - building a circuit.

He earned reward time and played restaurant with his friends - he was the cook in a busy kitchen!

What are the plans for Carol's birthday?

– Mike

Figure A.1 Sample Communication book entry. Image by Michael A. Murray.

Index

For Product Safety Concerns and Information please contact our EU representative GPSR@taylorandfrancis.com
Taylor & Francis Verlag GmbH, Kaufingerstraße 24, 80331 München, Germany

www.ingramcontent.com/pod-product-compliance
Ingram Content Group UK Ltd.
Pitfield, Milton Keynes, MK11 3LW, UK
UKHW022313250926
475702UK00046B/761
9781032218939